T0171685

"Dedicated to Rear Admiral John S. Christiansen,
Navy Cross 1944, warrior, leader, and mentor, and to
Chief Petty Officers Ivan Cansler and Kenneth Nichols,
whose patience and understanding exemplified
the values, visions, and virtues of authentic leaders.

TRANSFORMING!

HOW
MANAGERS
BECOME LEADERS

LEADERSHIP STORIES
FROM THE MILITARY, BUSINESS,
AND EDUCATION

RESOURCES
FOR GROUP FACILITATORS
AND LEADERSHIP DEVELOPMENT

KENNETH BREAUX

Order this book online at www.trafford.com
or email orders@trafford.com

Most Trafford titles are also available at major online book retailers.

Printed in the United States of America.

ISBN: 978-1-4907-1278-9 (sc)
ISBN: 978-1-4907-1279-6 (hc)
ISBN: 978-1-4907-1367-0 (e)

Library of Congress Control Number: 2013916125

Trafford rev. 10/04/2013

 www.trafford.com

North America & international
toll-free: 1 888 232 4444 (USA & Canada)
fax: 812 355 4082

Acclaim for Transforming

"As a member of management for a Fortune 500 organization, leadership and team-building are two attributes that I am constantly striving to enhance in my role(s). By applying the principles identified in this publication, I have become more effective as a leader. The applications are beneficial to the first-time supervisor, the senior executive, and every level in between."

**Michael Brooks, General Manager—
Dallas Metroplex MRF, Waste Management Inc.**

"In this impactful and insightful book retired U.S. Navy Commander Ken Breaux draws from his considerable military experience to bring stories of true leadership to life. Business leaders and those wishing to become business leaders will gain a valuable look into what separates true leaders who inspire from mere managers in these pages. I highly recommend this book as a teaching aid to any organization."

**Don Jordan, PE—Plant Manager,
Georgia-Pacific Gypsum, LLC**

"I've just had the pleasure of reading Ken Breaux's monograph on leadership. In clear and succinct language written for a general audience, Ken artfully illustrates that leadership is a skill that can be learned and applied by everyone from day laborers to chiefs of state. In fact, through a blend of personal anecdotes and case studies of historical figures, Ken delivers a unique perspective on leadership development.

The leadership lessons he learned from a co-worker he met while on a summer job as a member of a construction crew while still a teenager, resonate as strongly as lessons Ken derives from case studies highlighting leaders like General Norman Schwarzkopf and other historic figures.

Tomes on leadership fill business library bookshelves. As a rule they share the common feature of offering prescriptions for effective leadership. Ken Breaux has taken a different tack, instead of offering aphorisms and formulae, he invites readers into conversations. In providing this framework for conversations about moral, accountable, ethical leadership Ken makes an invaluable contribution to the corpus of leadership literature."

Fred Passman PhD., President, BCA Inc.

(Dr. Fred Passman is an industrial microbiologist. He has held numerous leadership positions in professional and religious communities. Dr. Passman retired from the US Navy after 31 years combined reserve and active duty service. During his Navy career he served six tours of duty as a commanding officer.)

"The subject of Leadership is a daunting, challenging and sometimes misunderstood subject or task which is totally teachable and learnable.

There is no perfect Leadership style for all the people all the time, but only a working leadership style when applied toward a targeted group of people in certain circumstances or conditions.

Ken takes a quite unique, bold and very innovative approach in providing teaching materials adapted from real stories and life experiences while allowing instructors and learners to reach their own conclusions and solutions."

Dr. Joe Hsieh, P.E. ConocoPhillips Global Projects Quality Manager and Adjunct Professor—Houston Community College, Mathematics and Natural Sciences

"Leading great talent is always a challenge for all businesses. "Transforming" combines practical, tested methods and philosophies with a variety of thought provoking and stimulating case studies to implement grass-roots leadership styles and techniques. Have your critical thinking skill hats on!"

David S, Burr, CAPT USN (Ret.), Coordinator Airport Operations Support, United Airlines

"If people were born Leaders, the USMC could pin a bar on their collars without further ado.

While some people may possess the innate qualities of leadership acquired from family or society at large, most people are not born Leaders. Leadership is a skill that can be taught by study and practice. Indeed, it is imperative that Leaders continually hone their "craft" in order to maintain their "edge" whether it be in the marketplace or on the battlefield.

In this vein, Cdr. Kenneth Breaux, USN Ret, has written an excellent instructional text that should be on the bookshelf of every Leader. Filled with examples of real life situations, the book seeks to stimulate discussion of what a Leader might do under different situations. This book provides an excellent tool for use by those who wish to be leaders, and those seeking to develop new leaders for their organizations."

Paul Evans is a Deputy Sheriff with the San Diego County Sheriffs Department in San Diego, CA.

CONTENTS

FOREWORD

Leadership of people is a high calling. Few have an adequate understanding of it; fewer still are able to put it into practice. It is not science, nor can one practice it as a set of mechanistic principles. It is above all, an art form, but it does have certain first principles from which we can derive its application. People, living, breathing humans, are true partners with their leaders. Authentic leaders create followers and teams that outperform others who superficially seem equal. True leaders envision people as the fuel of the enterprise. They bring its vision to life whether in a market, a battle in war, or a classroom.

Our external environment changes at a rate more rapid than any time in recorded history. Technology drives all manner of events with dizzying speed. While all these events surround and confound us, the one constant is human nature. Peoples needs and attitudes change somewhat, but the core of human nature is intact. The events in the narratives herein are as applicable now as they were 2,000 years ago. One of the great weaknesses of mankind is that we seem destined to commit the mistakes of the previous generation in our own. We should do well to remember that it is not history that repeats, but human nature, or perhaps, the history of human nature.

We choose to be leaders or managers. It is an individual choice. It requires truth and courage to be a leader. There are no substitutes for those two first principles. They enable us to become leaders in whatever arena we are in. And leadership does not require position or authority. It can be performed by persons in whatever circumstance they find themselves, in an appointed position or even a chance encounter. Leadership is a process of becoming, wherein we decide to embrace the concepts of the leader as opposed to the traditional institutional appointment. We must understand the concept of following before we can become leaders; for it is in following that we can best begin the process of understanding what constitutes a leader. It is a simple path, but one also filled with challenge. Leaders change things. They ask questions. They seek to pull, and not push. Have you ever tried to push a string?

Participating in the discussions in this volume or merely reading them will not create a leader in you. But if it awakens in readers the importance and nature of leadership and the desire to pursue them, then it has satisfied the objectives of this writer. Leaders never "arrive". They are always tuning, adjusting, listening, creating, and changing the environment of their work for the better.

PREFACE

"The commander must try, above all, to establish a personal and comradely contact with his men, while at the same time not giving away an inch of his authority."

General Irwin Rommel

As a young man, I made the decision during college that I would enter the Navy upon graduation in 1966. I was raised in a small town in Southwest Louisiana. My travel experience was limited. I spent twelve years in Catholic schools and there first learned about discipline and the sobering fact that all actions had consequences. My education in the Christian Brothers tradition made the military much easier. Discipline and authority were a daily experience, but never oppressive, and with those academic disciplines came a significant exposure to the teaching of virtues and respect for others.

My motives for joining the Navy were several. The flat prairie of Southwest Louisiana only encouraged my desire to see more of the world's geography. My first visit to the Gulf of Mexico was an epiphany. Just seeing the expanse of water and knowing that by setting out on that liquid road I could find the rest of the world was inspiring. I had also had the experience of an uncle, my dad's only brother, who had served with distinction as an infantry officer in Normandy as an example, and several other uncles who had served also.

The men who were senior Navy leaders at the time I joined had all been tested in the crucible of World War II. They were not only tested in battle, but in the practicalities of daily leadership of men. They had seen it all, from aerial combat to surface battles and submarine warfare, and there was a certain calm about them, even in the midst of dangerous operations and daily stress. But the most valuable aspect of their character was their attitude toward the men they led. These veterans walked the fine line that true leadership requires, the balance between good order and discipline and the ability to instill a paternal and protective atmosphere toward their men. They inspired us to achieve because they believed in us, and because we wished to please them. Above all, we trusted them. We learned what it was to become a follower.

This is not to say that every leader under which I served was perfect, nor was every commander an exemplary figure of leadership. The military is a cross section of any society. It contains people in the same proportions as found in society. But after a time in the ranks, there is a process which gradually finds the chaff, and for the most part, the people who really know how to lead tend to rise.

The examples of military leadership in this book come from a variety of sources. Some are from my own experiences, others from family members, and still more from reading military history. I wanted to write this account because after leaving the military I always looked for the indicators of leadership. They were not easy to find in the civilian world. The culture was strikingly different, but different in ways that the person who never served would not believe. I experienced real teamwork in the Navy, and witnessed more acts of leadership that inspired than I ever have in civilian life. To me, the quote by General Rommel epitomizes the difficulty faced by leaders. Leadership is not easy. It's about balancing competing values while struggling to maintain the objectives of the organization, and paying attention to people and their needs.

I have not had the leadership experiences of great men. I have experienced leadership success and leadership failure. But I have been a student of leadership, and it is as a student that I was motivated to develop this teaching tool for prospective leaders.

The cases presented in this volume are predominantly military and business, and a small sampling from the education community. Discerning readers and facilitators of the process will note that the environment is less important than the universal nature of the application. Leadership, whether it takes place in the military, business, or education, possesses certain characteristics which are universal across cultures, languages, and organizations. Human nature is a universal and timeless phenomenon, and leadership addresses that quality regardless of the culture or environment.

In the typical organization, people are promoted to supervisory positions for many reasons. Rarely are those promotions made because the person is a superior leader. Often those doing the promoting have no experience in leadership themselves. It is up to the new supervisor to learn leadership on their own. The person being promoted is usually selected because they are expected to fulfill the impersonal requirements of the transactional paradigm, not the humanistic elements of the transformational paradigm. We will address the issues of leadership not through the typical platitudes but rather through action. The reader will learn how action becomes leadership when the informed and prepared leader utilizes a leadership process plan and carries it out.

Leadership will be illustrated in narratives. While these are case studies, they are focused primarily at the social level, between people and their leaders and not at the level of strategy which are the focus of most case studies. We will experience events which occurred in war and peace, business and education, and we will learn how leaders reacted in both positive and negative manners. This is not a "how to lead" treatise. It is an attempt to draw leaders, new and old, into a serious examination and discussion of leadership, what it is, how it works, and why we should understand its potential. We spend more time at work than with family. If we spend that time in an organization that does not value our efforts, then we work for nothing except money. We face the daunting prospect of institutions which are sick in structure and social norms. These groups range from government to small businesses and occupying places in these organizations contributes to a diminished work productivity, a hindrance to family life, and a threat to once revered institutions.

Each potential leader will examine various facets of the lessons observed in this book. Each will bring their own challenges, bias, and conclusions to the study of leadership. In the end they will hopefully apply those lessons to their own lives and work. High on the list of lessons learned should be two factors. The first is courage. As Winston Churchill observed, "Courage is rightly esteemed the first of human qualities . . . because it is the quality which guarantees all others". (The same quote is also attributed to Aristotle) The second is truth. Truth is always available to the leader, but not always applied. Without courage truth dies an obscure death. Truth waits, a tool with a sharp edge and a sure effect, for leaders of courage to claim it. Courage and truth are the two essential tools of the leader.

ACKNOWLEDGEMENTS

Some years ago when I first discussed the idea of this project with Dr. Tim Carroll of the University of South Carolina, he raised the question of selecting the most effective pedagogy to deliver a leadership book. It was Tim who came up with the idea of a tool based on generating discussion for participants in a group environment. I owe him greatly for that advice. Don Jordan, P.E. has been supportive of the concept since the beginning and his enthusiasm and encouragement has provided much needed morale boosts. My late friend Harry Friedman helped to refine the concept of teaching versus learning regarding leadership. Lynn McCue provided an early critical review of the material, as did Dr. Fred Passman, Dr. Joe Hsieh, David Burr and Paul Evans. Eric Kirkpatrick provided critical comments on the text development, and also created a great cover design.

INTRODUCTION

WHAT IS LEADERSHIP AND WHY IS IT NECESSARY?

Leadership is social, situational, and historical. It is social, because it defines a particular relationship between people, situational, because a person is judged by how they react in a crisis or event requiring leadership values, and historical, because while leadership is frequently recognized in an instant, it is established in retrospection.

Leadership is an often misunderstood, certainly rarely wholly understood attribute of *character*. As such, it is often neglected, especially in the world of business and commerce. The place where this attribute of character has traditionally been strongest has been in the military establishments of the world and in certain situations where athletes have been led by those who have this attribute. Perhaps because of this, it has acquired a certain mystical quality. As those who have served in the military dwindle in numbers, this attribute is in danger of being lost. We are losing the "greatest generation", and with it, the ethos they brought back from their campaigns. And our modern athletes are largely reduced to entertainers who work for enormously high salaries. So what is leadership? How will we define it?

At the heart of any discussion of leadership lies a discussion of the transactional model or the classic management model. This is studied in basic business courses, and defines the tasks of the manager regardless of business type. The term "transactional model" came into use some years ago, but it is actually a very old model. Used in this sense, transactional means that there is a minimum contractual agreement between worker and corporation. Employee John Doe comes to work for the company and earns "X" amount of money for certain tasks "A, B, C". That's the bottom line. The transactional model has specific elements which can be organized, catalogued and measured. These are:

STAFFING/ PLANNING/ ORGANIZING/ DIRECTING/ CONTROLLING

The "bottom line" definition of a manager can be defined by these tasks. The person in business who aspires to simply manage is satisfied by their fulfillment of the classic roles of a manager. A manager is a business functionary, one who completes certain tasks. These tasks are well known by anyone who either takes a course in business or simply discovers them on their own. These are discrete tasks. Their completion can be measured. This fact places them in the classification of science, or perhaps accounting. Their overall effect is usually gauged by profitability and they are very specific. In the management model, the people are the means to the end, not specific elements of the model. Thus people, just like land and money, are often thought of as a renewable resource. They are renewable through termination and replacement. They are not essential to the model by any other means. Further, this model is restrictive, and highly dependent upon job descriptions. This rigidity forces the novice manager to become a sort of overseer. In this mode, young managers and old alike often see their role as enforcers. They believe it necessary to find fault with their subordinates. They become obsessed with the functions of directing and controlling. The classic management model is useful in those situations that are task oriented and highly detailed, but outside of those it can be stifling. It is useful in calibrating the organization from a financial point of view, and in fact can and should coexist with a leadership-oriented approach. To change a culture by transformational leadership, the building blocks of the transactional model must be in place and firmly established. Without the attributes of direction and control, a culture cannot be transformed.

ELEMENTS OF THE ORGANIZATION

The organization too, can be defined as having structure and specific elements. These are typically three; accounting/finance and quantitative, organizational structure, and the behavioral element. Some management specialists have looked at the balance of these three. They have compared them to a three-legged stool. The balance of the enterprise is on the seat of the stool. The enterprise needs a combination of all three, in concert and cooperation with each other. If this is not present, the enterprise becomes unbalanced and weakened. Shorten or lengthen any of the legs, and bad things can happen. Too much focus on people is just as bad as too much focusing on profits. Leadership exists along a spectrum. At the far left end are the functional and mechanical principles of management, the transactional model and its tasks. At the far right end is inspirational and transformational leadership. At that end lies the emotional territory of the human spirit. Leadership lifts the spirit. It is capable of a great deal. And most managers stay away from it because they cannot *measure it*, yet that is its greatest attribute, that it has no limits. Someone once said that managers work from the bottom, meaning the bottom line, and leaders work from the top, from a higher principle and ethos.

People affect each of the three elements in different ways, but always as people, with their infinite variability, often challenging and sometimes vexing personalities. The philosopher Zeno said that "People are all the same, they're different".[1] For the manager or supervisor who prefers pure stability and predictable environments, this is a problem. For the manager or supervisor who looks at people and says that each of them possesses the most powerful computer ever built, the one between their ears, there can be a different outcome.

THE LEADERSHIP MODEL

The leadership model is fundamentally different. It does not replace the management model, but superimposes an ethos over it. This model has its people at the center, and though it calls for the manager to fulfill the same discrete tasks as the management model, it imposes another higher calling. The leader is a manager, to be sure. But he must also be a developer and enabler of his people. This function of developing and enabling is difficult. It calls for the manager to step outside the comfortable confines of a thoroughly described management model and assume greater responsibility. But it has great potential. Through leadership, the manager taps emotional reserves not addressed in the supervisory functions of the management model. Leaders concentrate on what are often contemptuously called "soft skills." These are motivating, developing, and communicating with people. In this territory of leadership, there are few textbook solutions. The leader is called upon to improvise, and flexibility and spontaneity become important. A key element of leadership is the ability and desire to both listen and empathize. This alone often begins the process of unlocking the personal reservoir of emotion, character traits, and skills that can lead to greater performance. Leadership is not important for that reason alone. It is important because most of us spend the greater portion of our lives at the workplace, not with our families or friends. Our emotional health is often driven by our workplace. Psychiatrists have long recognized a condition called "folie a deux". This translates as "shared madness".[2] Spend too much time with someone with character defects and you acquire them. An oppressive leader can create a climate that is unhealthy. But a leader who is too receptive, too empathetic, may also acquire the unwholesome traits of his followers.

There is an old army maxim which says that the duty of an officer is to carry water for his troops. This addresses another characteristic of the leader. In order to see his people succeed, the leader must act as their enabler. This implies that many things are required of him. First he must know himself and his people. He must know what their difficulties are. He must understand them in depth, and it is better if he is there firsthand. By doing this he also learns, and in the process of learning he solves problems that he would not have solved otherwise. You cannot lead, or learn, from the rear. Contrast this with the management model in its overseer or supervisory mode. The implication there is that I know your job better than you, and I am here to find fault with the way you perform. The great difference between the two is that the leadership model is supportive in nature. "What do you need to get it done?" It is the job of the leader to ask that question. If he is lacking in humility, it may never get asked. If it is never asked, the subordinate assumes the worst. He thinks the boss doesn't care, that he only wants results. In this scenario, the organization cannot improve because it is not a learning and adaptive organization. If you don't learn, you make the same mistakes over and over. It is not history that repeats itself, but rather human nature. There is another lesson of great importance here. It is that discipline and regulations cannot exist without some form of nurturing on the personal level.

> "In times of crisis, individuals discover unsuspected strengths and reveal a capacity for bravery, endurance, generosity and loyalty beyond all expectations . . . sometimes capabilities remain simply because the circumstances of life do not evoke them . . . but sometimes the gifts have been buried by early defeats and harsh treatment, or layered over by cynicism or held inactive by self doubt . . . the battles we wage are not just exercises in compassion. They are battles for the release of human talent and energy."
>
> John Gardner

If there is anything good to come out of war, disease, tragedy, it is defined as above. We are humans . . . we are capable of great things. We are the only organism that we know of to have planned to leave our own ecosystem and traveled to another. We cannot be defined by job descriptions, or limited by another's idea of our own limitations. The organizations that succeed dramatically are those that tap the human potential. They seek to *develop* their human resources, not merely replace them.

The definition of a leader is somewhat straightforward, but the definition of leadership is more elusive. We tend to use the term rather freely when referring to persons of prominence in a field of endeavor, such as politics, sports, or business. James Macgregor Burns, a great management theorist, applies this definition to leaders; "Leadership over human beings is exercised when persons with certain motives and purposes mobilize institutional, political, psychological, and other resources so as to arouse, engage, and satisfy the motives of followers."[3] True enough as stated in context, but can we accept that definition in all cases? By that definition, would we classify Hitler or Osama Bin Laden as great leaders? Does it simply depend on our perspective, our particular point of view, and the accident of timing or our specific motivations? Once we find a leader who can pull us along toward our goals, does anything else matter? Issues of values and ethics are difficult to define. The above definition is workable but needs clarification for the situation. Most followers would place a condition of values on Burns' definition. By that qualification, we might eliminate such leaders as Hitler and others from our hall of fame for leaders, even though they fulfill certain elements of the description nicely. If we are going to follow, and follow with complete conviction, we tend to look for the personal ethics of a leader. The element of charisma is often used to frame the actions of leaders, especially those in the public eye. James H. Toner, a professor of ethics at the Air War College and a frequent contributor to military journals, offers another more precise, tightly woven definition. Toner contends that a better definition is . . . "leadership inspires appropriate conduct beyond the expectable."[4]

Pay particular attention to the verb he uses. Leadership *inspires*. We've established that the basis of most leadership has a foundation in the transactional basis of the organization. But we also know that to go beyond, to transform and change culture, we need to address more than the pure contractual terms of transaction. In the simple transactional culture, perhaps task dependent and very specific, leadership is sometimes challenging, but it is no less needed there than in other environments. There is a wealth of range in the term "appropriate conduct" too. To inspire requires much beyond the transactional. Toner goes further and expands his definition to include that the inspiration produced by transformational leaders includes positive and productive influence. Influencing alone is not sufficient.

THE INFLUENCE PYRAMID

FIGURE 1

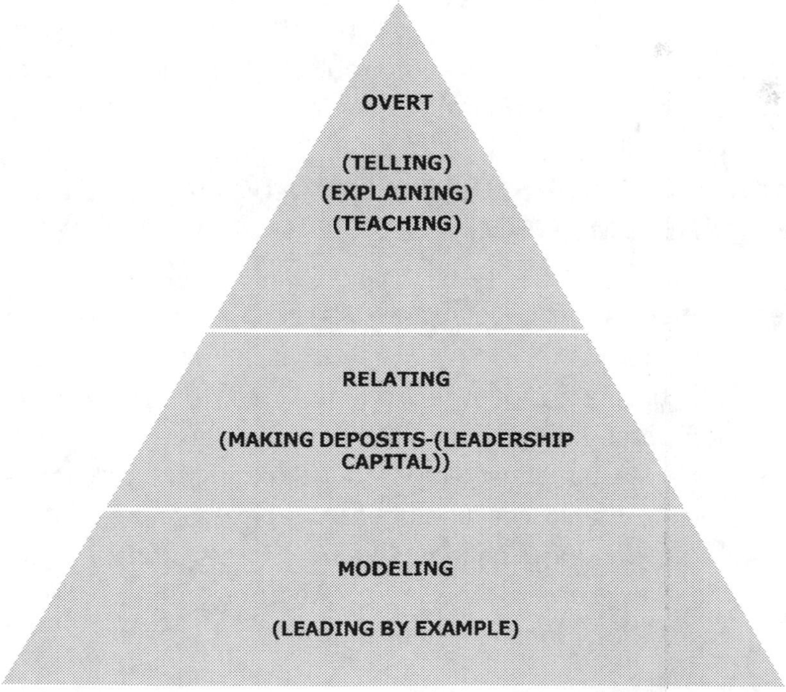

OVERT

(TELLING)
(EXPLAINING)
(TEACHING)

RELATING

(MAKING DEPOSITS-(LEADERSHIP CAPITAL))

MODELING

(LEADING BY EXAMPLE)

THE BALANCED PARADIGM

The acceptance of the paradigm of transformational leadership does not lead us to the conclusion that we can either always present ourselves as transformational leaders to the exclusion of the transactional. We will see examples of the combined paradigm in some of the cases in this book. The transactional is necessary and when properly applied it is supportive of the transformational. We need the basic framework of the transactional for this reason. What we must not do is to stop there, but to go on to understand and implement the functions of the transformational leader when the opportunity presents itself. It is also important to understand that leadership requires adaptive and flexible actions. Within a single organization, there may be an overall culture which also possesses several sub-cultures. Leaders must present themselves in a manner which is appropriate to each culture when they assume responsibility for the group. This is one of the primary reasons why leaders must get out into the field and spend time alongside their followers. By doing this we come to better understand the culture, work conditions, challenges and problems they face. We cannot lead well without this learning process.

TRANSACTIONAL VS. TRANSFORMATIONAL— THE PARADIGMS COMPARED

A desire for positive change above stability

- ○ Is it necessary to have a leader if the path is known to all? Organizations grow and improve through change. In a stable and purely transactional organization, change is uncomfortable, challenging, and unpleasant. The essence of transformation is change. In a rigid transactional paradigm, the ethic is always "this is how we do it, and this is how we have always done it". There is no desire to change.

A philosophy of leading people as opposed to managing work

- The completion of tasks and projects is the mission, the people are the enablers. "Mission First, People Always"

The formation of followers rather than subordinates

- Followers go willingly with a leader. Subordinates are ordered to do so.

A longer term vision, beyond the pursuit of immediate objectives alone

- The transactional calls for objectives to be met. This is proper, but the leader will develop a vision beyond the achievement of transactional objectives.

A proactive dynamism, not a reactive response

- If you can only react, you are driven by events, rather than driving events.

A search for the truth as it may exist, not what is currently accepted

- When you assume leadership of a new group, one of the very first things that must be done is to establish the truth. Are the members being led, or driven? Are the right people assigned to the tasks? Are they being treated fairly? No leader should assume that the truth is as presented to them. Leaders assuming responsibility for a group must determine that for themselves.

The knowledge that doing the right thing is greater than doing things right

- The right thing is the moral and ethical approach. Doing things right simply addresses the minimal transactional issues. Sometimes the right thing is hard, but it must be done if you wish to lead and transform. Sometimes the right thing goes against your own self interest, but in the longer term it is best.

A desire to transform

- If you do not believe that you can improve on the status quo, then you are probably not a leader. The desire and belief that you can do something better with the work before you is a necessary asset to transform the workplace. To do this you must have confidence in both yourself and the people you would lead.

A rejection of the transactional exchange as primary or the only criterion

- The transactional exchange, or work only for pay, is part of a necessary structure that must be present for the transformational to operate. But it is not the only condition for which most people work.

To persuade rather than to direct or order

- Traditional managers direct and order people. Transformational leaders persuade. They know that persuasion enables them to address the higher emotional gratification of the group and offers greater motivation to the members.

A drive to achievement and personal development for each of the team members rather than the group's transactional objectives alone

○ Leaders truly believe that each member of the team has value. They also have a desire to participate in the development of each member to the fullest extent possible within the constraints of the job and individual capability of the person involved.

An understanding of the use and proper time to accept risk

○ It is only in a perfect world that there is no risk. By risk we typically do not mean taking risks with safety issues. But we do mean taking risks with policy issues or similar types of process challenges. If it is clear that by taking a risk to prove a point or solve a problem, and that such risk does not involve egregious violations of policy, then that is often not only permissible, but sometimes necessary. We will illustrate this with cases, but risk is in some measure, unavoidable.

A reliance on personal charisma rather than institutionally appointed status

○ Appointment does not make a leader. One has to earn the position. We earn the position of leader when we generate true followers. We earn it in many ways, but mostly by being someone who appeals to followers, who knows his job and that of his followers, and by acting in a manner that appeal to both the organization above and below his position.

An ability to appeal to deeper emotions above the transactional "head" or intellectual solutions

○ Napoleon said that emotions rule the world. Appealing to those emotions in an ethical and sensible manner is the work of the leader. Those passions enable the leader to achieve more from his followers than the mere "work for pay". Followers find in themselves deep resources beyond the transactional when led, not pushed or driven.

A keen appreciation of the importance of direction as opposed to detail

- While the "how we get there" is important, it is less important than if you are going to the wrong place. Direction must be established before the details of the "how".

An understanding that rules are used when you have no idea of what to do next; that they occasionally must be bent or even broken

- There are exceptions to this statement. One is safety. Safety rules should never be bent or broken. Neither should policies regarding alcohol or drug use. While leaders must be judicious in "bending or breaking" rules, they also should have the foresight and courage to know that if the breaking of a rule benefits the organization and violates no ethical or legal limits, it probably is a rule that should be removed from the policy manual.

A desire for achieving greater results as opposed to the maintenance of simple action to satisfy the transactional

- The transactional manager operates on the concept of trading "x" money for "y" work. The transformational leader has a vision of delivering more to both the organization and the follower. He does this by motivation and spreading his own passion for work to his followers.

The desire and ability to use conflict profitably and creatively

- The transactional paradigm avoids conflict because it disrupts the desired stability. The transformational leader embraces conflict because it is the reality. If it is there, it must be addressed. Avoiding conflict settles nothing, allowing dissent and possible solutions to remain unseen while affecting the group cohesion and goals.

The liberal use of credit for the achievements of followers

- ○ True leaders deem the giving of credit one of their most enjoyable activities. They are active and involved partners in the development and success of their followers.

The acceptance of responsibility or blame rather than passing it to followers

- ○ You may delegate authority, but you may never delegate responsibility.

The use of the team to facilitate decisions as opposed to using sole authority to make them

- ○ Often the traditional approach to management is to assume that one is there to find fault with, and correct, subordinates. Along with this attitude comes a companion attitude that if appointed, you are there to make all decisions. Nothing could be less effective or more dangerous. The people who do the daily work have an intimate knowledge of that work. You must know that work, and keep the communication open to those who are involved in it. You should almost never make a decision that will affect your team without first understanding how it will affect them. An important by-product of this process is that the leader achieves a group "buy-in" to the solution. This does not mean that there are never solutions or answers which you must make alone. There are those, but decisions that affect the group are often best first put to the group for suggestions.

The search for new and creative direction beyond the existing direction

- ○ It is important, even critical, to continually assess and reassess the direction of an organization. As external and internal events drive change, direction is often affected.

A passion for work superimposed above the desire for control

- ○ To control at the expense of passion is to simply work toward the transactional to the exclusion of leadership which transforms.

A global, not linear approach to the problem at hand

- ○ Leaders have to accomplish specific tasks, but those tasks must contribute to the vision that they and their own leaders have for the organization.

FIGURE 2

The following table is reprinted with credit to the University of Notre Dame

Subject	Leader	Manager
Essence	Change	Stability
Focus	Leading people	Managing work
Have	Followers	Subordinates
Horizon	Long-term	Short-term
Seeks	Vision	Objectives
Approach	Sets direction	Plans detail
Decision	Facilitates	Makes
Power	Personal charisma	Formal authority
Appeal to	Heart	Head
Energy	Passion	Control

Culture	Shapes	Enacts
Dynamic	Proactive	Reactive
Persuasion	Sell	Tell
Style	Transformational	Transactional
Exchange	Excitement for work	Money for work
Likes	Striving	Action
Wants	Achievement	Results
Risk	Takes	Minimizes
Rules	Breaks	Makes
Conflict	Uses	Avoids
Direction	New roads	Existing roads
Truth	Seeks	Establishes
Concern	What is right	Being right
Credit	Gives	Takes
Blame	Takes	Blames

WHY START HERE?

If you can learn to follow, and to be able to discern which leaders are truly good and effective, you have begun to learn the process of leading. If you enter a bookstore and check out the shelves, you'll see hundreds of books about leadership. Many of these will be about the lives of business leaders who've risen to prominence in large, well-known companies. Of the thousands who will buy those books, a handful will rise to the top of the types of organizations described in their pages. But the bulk of business in the world takes place in smaller organizations, especially those groups within the larger whole. It's in those organizations that the greatest need exists for leaders. It's in those organizations too that the greatest number of new leaders waits to develop. Following the military model, we see that no one begins at the top. Generals and Admirals all started at the bottom and learned to lead on the way up. Despite the fact that the structure of military organizations is hierarchical and highly structured, the best of their leaders are transformational. They learn to manage, and to lead, at the small unit level. Those who do not first succeed at the small unit levels will rarely rise very high. At the level of corporals, sergeants, lieutenants and captains, leadership is the major focus. At the levels above that, the focus tends more to management and issues of strategy. The capitalist system has no inherent ethic to support it. Money is the object. Any ethic that works its way into the system is placed there by people of honor. There are the hard-charging take-no-prisoners types who compare capitalism to warfare. Few if any of these have experienced combat. Fewer still will take the time to listen to the argument that there is such a concept as enlightened self-interest. Yet there are many examples of this, even in the world of corporate give and take.

In this discussion of leadership we concentrate on the distinction between strategic leadership that occurs at a very high level, and the leadership of people in small groups at the operating level. The volume of production of books regarding leadership at strategic levels seems unending. I've always found this a sort of disconnect. When and where do we address the fact that true leadership begins at the lowest level in the organization? Many of these books assume the premise that great leaders have done it all by themselves. It is true that there is a relationship between the strategic and the operational leader. It's necessary and critical to have this relationship. But without someone to do the fighting, the general has nothing to command. Colonel Dandridge Malone wrote a classic book on small unit leadership in the 1980's after he retired from the US Army. In his "Small Unit Leadership—A Commonsense Approach" he discusses the levels and types of leadership.[5] Generals he says, concentrate forces for the battles. Colonels direct those forces, and Captains through Sergeants fight the battle. The population of workers at the operating level is the target of this book. They are the closest to the action. They are the delivery drivers, factory floor workers, sales people and others most responsible for the delivery of products and services on a daily basis. The logic is simple. Before you accept responsibility to direct and concentrate forces, you should learn how to fight. In "One Bullet Away-The Making of a Marine Officer", author

Nathaniel Fick describes his experiences as a Marine in Afghanistan and Iraq as he led a platoon into combat[6]. Fick truly loved leading his Marines, and found that he could engage in combat and kill the enemy as necessary. When it came time to make a decision about a career in the Marine Corps, Fick opted out despite a solid record of performance in two combat deployments. His reason was that he understood the requirements of leading at higher levels. Those who direct the forces will bring about the deaths of Marines, and Fick said that he would not be able to do that. In his words; "Great Marine commanders, like all great warriors are able to kill that which they love most-their men. It's a fundamental law of warfare. Twice I had cheated it. I couldn't tempt fate again." In two deployments, Fick had never lost a fellow Marine. We can't know how many officers and Non Commissioned Officers (NCO's) leave the military for similar reasons. The lesson in Fick's reasoning is that true leadership creates a bond between people. In the civilian world, we will not face the same challenge that senior military leaders do as they ascend, although we often may encounter many civilian leaders who consider ascending to the top a blood sport. In that world, we see a number of CEO's who come to their new roles with attorneys and CPA's and structure a deal that makes them wealthy even while their organizations are dying. These are false leaders. They care little for those they affect. They are not authentic, and probably have never known leadership in its truest sense. We may not be able to form a bond in the civilian workplace with the same intensity as is found in combat. What we can do is to transform the workplace through leadership so that those who do the "fighting" are fulfilled by the work they do.

LEADERSHIP: ART OR SCIENCE?

There are many myths associated with the term "leadership". There are implications that one can choose a pattern of leadership, and that everyone possesses some form of leadership. There are Gen. Patton's, Coach Lombardi's, Ross Perot's, and countless others we call leaders from all walks of life. Much of the training given to business students and MBA's involves quantitative subjects. Higher math, accounting, operations research, statistical quality control methods etc., occupy much of our business curricula. We certainly need to pay attention to these things if we are to have a "bottom line" which allows us to survive. The overemphasis of these things however, in some cases keeps us from utilizing the full potential of our people. The human being is the most adaptable and creative organism on the earth. People are what will ultimately differentiate between similar bottom lines and really successful and adaptable organizations. Things happen fast in today's organizations, not unlike 60 minutes of professional football between two more or less evenly matched teams. Using the technology we possess to determine the bottom line is good. Computers and sophisticated software programs give us the ability to know financial situations daily if we desire. The attitudes of the people are the only things that can change those numbers. Under skilled leadership capable of motivating people, the turnaround is achieved. So what are leaders, as defined by businesses? Stephen Covey, in his book "Seven Habits of Highly Effective People", offers a good example.[7] He talks about the difference between leaders and managers. Given the task of building a road through a forest, the managers assemble teams, train tree cutters, measure the daily progress, etc. Some leader climbs to the top of a tree, takes a long look forward, and shouts "Wrong forest". Vision is important, so is motivational outlook. Courage plays a big part. In short, leaders cannot afford to get too far bogged down in the micro-details. The bottom line numbers can be seductive, even comforting. But the trend, the pulse of the people is sometimes more important. Leaders, like good coaches, often get more done with less talent than anyone else. Coaches and leaders must also recognize that they are not the only leaders in their organizations. They must have the ability to select the players who will motivate others. The job cannot be done alone, and good leaders are not afraid to recognize others. The science of management is easily defined, with plenty of yardsticks to measure performance. We must continue to manage, using those skills, but we must realize that we need to practice the pursuit of leadership as well. The art of leadership is less well defined, and the human spirit more complex and often vexing and challenging than some managers would like. The workplace has a massive human need. Money and benefits supply a critical part of that need, the basic issues of survival and security. The remainder of that need must be supplied by leaders, artists who motivate and shape the attitudes of humans, the most adaptable and ingenious organism on the planet. The organizations which supply that very human need will not only be the survivors, but the "thrivers", of the future. The choice belongs to the manager. He or she can be a "number mechanic", producing a change in the bottom line by the next quarter simply by firing people and spending less money. Or they can choose the path of leadership. The person who works for a leader recognizes that person's leadership qualities, even if the leaders cannot articulate those qualities themselves. They recognize it, and they work a little harder, smarter, more creatively, without being told to, because they are being led, not herded or driven. And they succeed in spite of all manner of obstacles, often when they are told they cannot. These are the legacies of leaders.

CAN LEADERSHIP BE TAUGHT?

While definitions of the descriptive elements of leadership can be taught, the active elements of what makes a leader can probably best only be learned. This is probably paradoxical to you at first, but we will develop the process of learning leadership in a somewhat different approach. There are many things whose definition can be difficult to express. Love and beauty are two which come to mind. Beauty pleases the eye. Leadership lifts the spirit. It is difficult if not impossible to measure these attributes. Many times we find difficulty in describing these things, but we nevertheless know them when we experience them. There is a parallel process in learning leadership. In the foundation readings and cases we will describe both the descriptive elements of leadership and a framework for studying these elements. Those are discrete events and actions, and they can be taught. But we will take a different path in developing a learning process. All of the narratives we discuss are events that actually happened. In each of these narratives, the reader will see a "leadership moment" in action. In some of these, you will see what that learning (or teaching) moment was. In others you will note that the opportunity was missed. Experiencing failure can also be a great learning tool, and in these cases the reader may experience both success and failure vicariously. A great part of leadership is very often the result of seizing these moments to create a leadership experience that not only builds trust and credibility of the leader, but in so doing creates followers, not subordinates. Learning leadership requires exposure to the actual events, with the basis for logical-rational elements taught in the usual method. To that end you will find multiple narratives from the military, business, and education. While each event is specific to the environment in which it occurred, none of them are exclusive to other environments. The principles of leadership are universals, regardless of where they may be practiced.

HISTORY AND SITUATIONAL LEADERSHIP

> "There is no future, only the past occurring over and over, now".[8]
>
> Eugene O'Neill

There are many discussions of historical situations in this writing. That's because I believe that the above quote is a living doctrine. What it means, broken down, is that there are truly very few unique or special situations. History is replete with examples of that, from the early Greeks to the recent presidents. None of us should be so vain as to ignore the wisdom of the classical thinkers. It is often said that history repeats itself. This is true, in a limited sense. Humans make history, and human nature repeats endlessly its successes and failures.

It is very important to realize that there are really very few new ideas when it comes to leading people. The rules are simple. This does not mean that they are easy. Virtues like honesty, integrity, loyalty, are simple, are they not? But as we watch the news that emerges every day in our media, we see that the simplest of things are sometimes never fulfilled by politicians, professional people, and the ordinary man.

The cycle of failure repeats endlessly. The reason for this repetition is that most of us believe that the events that we face are unique. That is true in that perhaps we have never been in those situations before, but it is certain that someone else has. It is equally certain that in almost every instance, there is some precept, some basic and fundamental rule that applies to the situation. My experience in watching leaders, in being a follower, and leading others has been that the most common deficit found in leaders is that they fail to observe the basics. It's not the difficult, complex problems of leading that cause them to fail. It's more often that they have failed in the simple tasks, and in that failure they set themselves up for greater and more consequential failure because they have no solid foundation as a leader beneath them. Knowing the right thing to do is usually not difficult. It's doing what is right that is difficult. Often it requires us to sacrifice something, and that is not pleasant, but is often absolutely necessary. To know the right thing without acting toward it reflects a lack of courage.

MBA programs increasingly orient their students toward the quantitative. Many are slanted heavily toward operations research, finance, and higher math. But this seems inappropriate when we consider that we must lead people, not numbers. Numbers cannot be led; they have discrete and limited qualities. They do not get sick, have children, or interact with us. The trend to quantitative is further fueled by the ability of the PC to do balance sheets in nearly real-time, and to take the precision of our accounting to greater decimal places. Common sense among leaders is often not a very common phenomenon. Working the numbers is popular, and comforting. But over-emphasizing the quantitative factors sets the leader up for failure.

We also need to remember that leaders require followers. If we have not built up the leadership capital needed to sustain followers, when the trouble starts, they won't be there when we need them. And if we think that we don't need followers, then we have violated one of the elemental rules of leadership.

THE ARENA OF THE LEADER

OPEN SYSTEMS

As the world grew, technology accompanied its progress. In the 1950's biologist Ludwig von Bertalanffy developed the concept of open systems.[9] There are lots of academic theories centered on this concept but the bottom line is that the events within organizations are affected by the events surrounding them. If we consider the organization as the largest of groups, and then consider that groups existing within organizations are also affected, as are the people in the groups, we begin to see that the issue of organizations, groups, and people within is very complex and infinitely varied.

There are organizations in which people count for very little. The structure and position are where the power resides. There is little creative thought, if any, and rules are everything. If there is one thing that characterizes bureaucracies, it is that they attempt to simplify the events around them to conform to a system of rules and structure. There is a place for rules in every organization. The key is finding the place, the time, and the event that has the need and applying the rules. The transactional bureaucrat sees a rule in every situation, and if there is not one, he makes one. It's an easy way to avoid having to think. The thinking leader, however, sees opportunities not to make rules, but to earn leadership capital. It's not easy. It's often hard work, and involves getting into the issues that center around people. Remember that no matter how you structure an organization or what rules you develop, it will be people who occupy the structure and it will be people who are affected by the rules.

THE ORGANIZATION AS AN OPEN SYSTEM

FIGURE 3

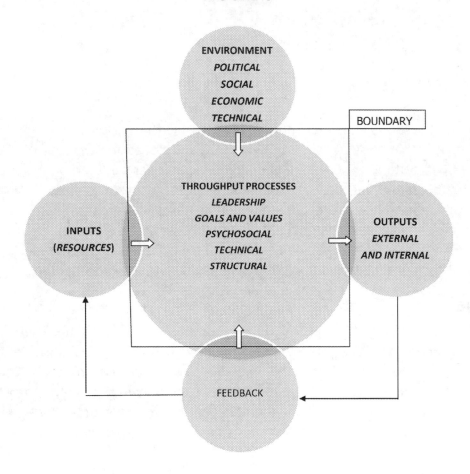

INPUTS

In the simplified graphic of the organization shown above, inputs can be external material resources such as steel or chemicals, but they also are represented by the human and technical resources of its members. Ideas, designs, and other resources are part of the input.

BOUNDARIES

These represent certain limitations on the organization. They can be ethical, legal, or social, or any number of restrictions imposed from external or internal sources. They can also be self imposed limits on the market the organization seeks to pursue. Subgroups within an organization may have different boundaries for each group.

THROUGHPUT PROCESSES

These processes represent the procedure in which the organization goes about producing goods and services. They can be physical processes such as construction, or intellectual processes.

FEEDBACK

Successful organizations and the groups within them seek and do not attempt to limit feedback. It can come from external sources such as customers or internal sources. A learning and self correcting organization has a good grasp on the need for feedback and knows how it must be used.

OUTPUTS

Outputs come in the form of finished product or service, and often also from critical internal reviews of performance by members of the organization. Both are valuable. Internal outputs can, if properly understood and vetted, can be used to improve performance in the learning organization.

ENVIRONMENT

Increasing organizations are subject to changes in the political environment of the arena in which they perform. Economic climate directly affects performance by accelerating or decreasing the generation of internal capital, and is the critical variable for success in competitive markets and capitalist economies. The short life span of technical advantages dictates the need for rapid response in technically oriented companies.

THE ORIGINS OF THE ORGANIZATION

In the Western World and much of the rest, organizations trace their hierarchical structure to the Roman Army and the Catholic Church. It was a form that worked, and as long as outside influences on those two institutions were stable and predictable, it worked well. It still does, if we can find any predictable and stable situations in which to place it, but there are limits to what it can accomplish. Those that most often come to mind are city and state governments that administer functions such as issuing driver licenses and providing other task specific services. The first test of those hierarchical structures was during the Industrial Revolution. In that period of time when the nature of business changed from small merchant societies and subsistence farming, the presence of a hierarchical structure allowed emerging organizations to grow and prosper. The goods and services they offered were revolutionary, and the changes they introduced to the society of those times were enormous. What has changed, and dramatically so, is the rate of change that affects organizations in current times. You might say that change has changed. Let's take a few historical examples to illustrate the point that change took a lot of time until the last hundred years or so. In the 4th and 3rd Millennia before the birth of Christ, now popularly called "BCE" or Before Christian Era, the Egyptians had a sophisticated system of weights and measures. That system endured until the advent of mechanical scales. Where before, the lowest level of accuracy was about the equivalent of one ounce, mechanical scales and balances now allow a degree of precision in fractions of ounces. Modern technology now calculates weights to the unit known as the Yoctogram, or one Septillionth of one ounce. Where early people calculated dates and time by the movement of celestial bodies, when and if they were visible, Harrison's mechanical chronometer in the 1700's gave timekeeping a new level, down to within seconds in a minute. And in 1955, the first atomic standard clock was deemed to be accurate to within one second in 300 years. Presently the National Institute of Standards calculates the latest atomic standard to be accurate to within one second in 1,400,000 years.

In 1947, Bell Labs invented the first transistor. In 1953, Motorola began production of transistors for low cost commercial use. In 1957, the sales of transistors had reached 100 million dollars annually. By the time that Jack Kilby developed the first integrated circuit in 1957; the race was on in earnest. The first computer built using integrated circuits made its debut in 1961, and by the year 2000, sales of the semiconductor industry reached 200 billion dollars.

Interesting history, but what does it have to do with business? Almost everything and anything in the world of business depends on these devices and their corresponding accuracy. Transportation and financial transactions, computing, manufacturing, electric power generation, aviation, space exploration and countless other fields all impact commerce with their developments. Remember the heartburn about the possible disasters centered on Y2K? But more importantly is the lesson that change is rapid and demanding. Businesses today are open systems, open to the external influences and pressures that are global, societal, task and culture related. And these changes occur at a dizzying frequency and impact the organizations dramatically, and often severely. The Roman Army and the Church of the middle Ages possessed a grip on the world of their times. These institutions lasted centuries before they were impacted by change. Today, companies are either making change or being affected by it. The organizations of today sometimes have months before a new competitive technology thrusts them from emergence into survival. One of the most intriguing descriptions of change came from an address made by the late Admiral James Stockdale, who received the Medal of Honor for exemplary conduct during his confinement as a POW during the Vietnam War. In this address, delivered to the graduating class of Salve Regina College in Newport, Rhode Island, Stockdale identified traits he believed were possessed by those who occupied prominent and valued places in history. He concluded the address by talking about change. "The thin veneer of civilization that we know is precious . . . We could seat in this auditorium, a couple, man and wife, representing each generation of man since he acquired his present appearance and characteristics, about 50,000 years ago. There would be only about 800 couples . . . . The first 650 of the couples would have lived in caves; only the last 70 would have had effective means of communicating with their fellow man, only the last 6 would have ever seen a printed page." [10]

Hierarchy is still a useful component of the organization structure. But rigid hierarchy without the expectation of external influence is not practical in most profit making commercial endeavors today.

In the American business culture of the early 1900's, the values of the Industrial Revolution still held that the elements of production were land, labor, and capital. Labor was plentiful and workers were regarded as replaceable. The tasks were not particularly challenging, but rather monotonous, and the average worker was not intellectually challenged. Managers and supervisors held all the information, and workers were poorly informed as to the processes and especially as to the financial situation of the company. Peter Drucker, the famous management theorist, first coined the term "knowledge worker" to describe the phenomenon of workers who had intellectual capital and more intimate knowledge of their workplace. Some economists and business researchers now contend that the knowledge worker as broadly defined outnumbers other workers by a huge margin. If so, that knowledge comes with a challenge.

There are management theorists who contend that the type of organization defines its structure, that structure shapes and molds behavior, and behavior sets the parameters for performance. They believe that the flow of these elements from organization to structure to behavior and finally performance is predictable. If proven, this seems to support the open systems theory, at least to some extent. All of this information is background for the new supervisor or manager who hopes to lead. It is useful to know and characterize the type of organization in which you work. This information tells you something of the culture of the organization, and provides guidelines for your own behavior. As an emerging leader you should be concerned with the interaction you have with your immediate work group. For you, that is where the action lies.

CHANGE IN CONTEXT-EVERYTHING IS DIFFERENT BUT LITTLE IS CHANGED

It's true . . . everything is different but little has changed. That is to say, nothing regarding leadership and people has changed. It's important to make the distinction between external change and people themselves. Many managers fail to do this. They do not realize that the change brought about by technology and markets, products, and services required really has very little to do with the process of leadership. Those external changes may require different responses in a technical sense, or in product development, but leadership and human nature can be traced across millennia without significant differences over time. The principles of leadership and the core of human behaviors are constants. Machiavelli's famous treatise on politics in medieval times, The Prince, is read by MBA students today, and still retains its relevance. It's important to understand that humanity is the core of every organization today, and that humanity has not changed its attributes. We do know more about ourselves, at least from the perspective of psychological research, but beneath it all we are essentially unchanged. This unchanging core of attributes is at the heart of the leadership process. Future leaders should take heart in this fact. This quality of human nature is probably the only constant you will face in your future as a manager. It is the one thing you can count on to remain the same.

THE GROUP

Leadership revolves around the actions and reactions of people to each other, in a one-to-one relationship or a one-to-many relationship. Each of these encounter formats has somewhat separate and unique connotations. In general, we deal in this book with groups, in which the leader is the one and the group consists of the many. This is the typical starting point for new leaders and the structure in which most new leaders need the most guidance.

As an emerging leader, it's important for you to understand how groups work, and how you will interact with your task group as their leader. In the military model, we learn how the individual is brought into the system with its predictable structure and comprehensive indoctrination and "joining up" process. We cannot expect all civilian institutions to have such a process in place, but it is important to manage that process nevertheless. That requires that you as a leader have some process, however minimal, to assess candidates for entry into the group and to assure yourself and the group that they meet the job task standards and will integrate well into the group. By understanding how groups behave, leaders can build stronger groups, and they will be able to form cohesive groups where none exist. This group building should be a key goal of leaders. The processes of coaching, mentoring, recruiting, and sanctioning group members are all part of the leaders tasks as they strive toward building, nurturing, and sustaining their task group.

The term "group dynamics" was first used in the 1950's, and it means simply the way that people in groups interact with each other and how groups behave in general.[11] We've already established that the organization as a whole is an open system. Groups are also open systems, and have many of the same forces acting on them as do the larger organization to which they belong.

THE GROUP AS AN OPEN SYSTEM

FIGURE 4

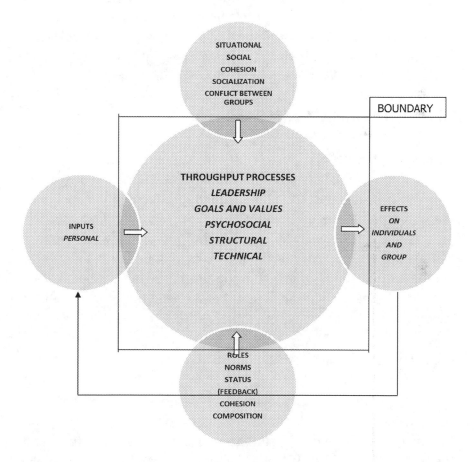

In the diagram seen above, you will see some new terms introduced. In broad terms though, we can start by defining inputs, throughput, and outputs. These are the same general characteristics we see in the definition of the overall organization as an open system.

INPUTS

In the group, these consist simply of the personal characteristics of each of the members and the leader, and the typical situation in which the group goes about its task assignments. In the military model, the personal characteristics of the members are traditionally defined very tightly, with each member having certain very specialized abilities and training. The area of situational characteristics however, is very fluid in the military model, with the group having perhaps dozens of different missions or task assignments in which the roles of individuals may vary.

THROUGHPUT PROCESSES

Structure in this context does not mean size or organizational form, but in the study of groups refers to the patterns that members develop in their interactions with other group members. In turn, the outcome of structure determines what kinds of processes the group will use to solve business problems or tasks to which they are assigned. The group may recognize that one member is the "go to" person for questions of a certain nature based on that member's experience. The member then assumes a role in the process pattern used by the group.

OUTPUTS

The outputs of a group consist of only two elements. These are the effects of the throughput processes on the individual, and the effects on the group. Training in skills is a desired output, and the will to deliver the skills is a factor of psychology and morale. In the military model, these outputs are measured, and we call these measurements "metrics". Operational Readiness Inspections are the US Navy's method of determining if a ship has met all the standards required to perform a successful combat deployment. In these inspections, every aspect of a ship's operational performance is measured against a standard for that class of ship. Gaps in the performance are noted and timelines are given for remedial action. As a group leader, you must determine what the metrics should be for your team. Sales managers for example, will hold the sales person to a quantitative metric. So many "cold calls" per day or week, so many appointments, or a specific volume of sales revenues.

INTERNAL OUTPUTS

The internal outputs of the group include motivation, satisfaction, and Knowledge, Skills, and Abilities. (KSA's)

EXTERNAL OUTPUTS

When we measure external outputs, we are typically concerned with issues such as service and its quality, general productivity, and the perception of the clients of our organization.

THE TUCKMAN MODEL—FORM-STORM-NORM-PERFORM

The Tuckman Model was first developed in 1965 by Bruce Tuckman.[12] Today it is used to describe the various stages through which group's progress. As a leader, it is useful for you to understand the basics of these processes. You can apply the same analysis to a small group, the overall organization, or sub-groups within each. It's necessary to have a performing group to reach corporate objectives and standards. But often it is necessary to revisit some of the stages along the way. The greater the outside forces acting on the group, the greater need for the stages to be revisited.

The original purpose of these stages was to define the logical sequences found in group development beginning from a zero point. But it should be apparent that things do not necessarily unfold in this order all of the time. Given the high level of mobility in the business environment, we might even argue that we are always in the process of forming and reforming, storming and re-storming, and norming and re-norming. Our performance requirements are typically ever-changing too. The stages are a bit more predictable when we examine a group newly begun, in which no one person is familiar with the others, and the objective is unknown at the time of formation.

In the forming phase, the members come together and begin the process of knowing each other. In this phase, it is important for the leader/supervisor to be the facilitator of the forming process. In the military model, some of the basic foundations for group formation and norms are developed in the joining phase. The group leader in that circumstance works from a well established set of rules and regulations. When the new military member reports for duty in their first working role, their leader has certain assurances that they come with a firm foundation of the organizations expectations and norms. Sometimes, especially in small businesses it isn't that straightforward. You may find yourself in the role of assessing training needs, and having to work with the Human Resources department in order to establish some basic requirements for entry into the group. In any event, it's important for the leader to use this opportunity to get to know their people, and to watch the interaction among members. The same process applies when a new member is inserted into an already performing group. It's necessary for the leader to know what type personality will best fit the existing group. In World War II, men new to the unit were often entering the group at a disadvantage. If the group had been through the forge of combat, the new man is seen as untested and perhaps unfit. This is especially true if he was to replace a soldier wounded or killed in action. The exceptional cohesion of such a group makes it difficult to break through. But cohesion, the unity of the group and their tendency to "stick together", is a goal of all good leaders. The military achieves cohesion through tradition, values, training, and shared experiences in which the unit not only survives but as a result comes together more solidly than before.

In the event known as storming, the group openly debates ideas such as the definition of their goal or how it should be approached. During this event tempers sometimes flare and personalities emerge for the leader to assess. Since we have stated that no group is ever completely static, storming may emerge each time a new project, goal, or idea is presented for the group to consider. Under the facilitation of a skilled group leader, this process may be tense, but the outcome is productive. This is often a great opportunity for the leader to observe each of the personalities and begin to understand their psychology. You can witness their attitudes toward each other, and their ability and willingness to present and defend their ideas. In a session of storming, the leader should facilitate by making sure the opportunity to contribute is given to every member. Sometimes people who are very reserved and quiet have no lack of ideas, but may have a reticence or shyness about speaking up. You need them all, not just the talkers.

In the norming process, teams have successfully come together and by this time, they have agreed on most of the goals and production values. The group and its leader may decide to formalize the rules, or norms. They may also be mature enough as individuals to work as a team without a great deal of formal structure. In any event, norming represents the time when the group has begun to work together, with or without formal rules, and is possessed with values, customs, and a work ethic. They understand their place in the larger organization, and have set goals to work toward group goals as well as strategic objectives. They are comfortable with each other, and with the work. My personal preference for the operative verb of this phase is "collaborative". A leader will know his group is fully through the norming events when he sees teamwork and collaboration.

When the teamwork begins and collaboration is evident, the group is in a performing phase. They know their jobs, and require little or no supervision. They also know the scope of the job, and may resort to a storming session when a task emerges which seems out of their scope or is a new task. When this occurs, a productive and performing group will seek the leader's guidance. The leader must facilitate the new storming session with the same care that he directed the earlier forming and storming encounters. Storming may occur each time a new task is introduced, or a new project is assigned. Re-norming is sometimes necessary to adapt to changing external or internal factors. All the above phases are dynamic. They occur with regularity when new people enter the group, or when people leave the group. Often the leader must account for a diminishing of performance, and restart the various processes to get the production values back into gear. It's part of what makes the leader and manager job so fulfilling. If you find this difficult, or think that it takes too much time, you probably need to assess your own performance as a leader. People, their sentiments and interactions in the daily workplace, are the job of the leader. Treat them well, understand and address their needs and abilities, and they will perform very well for you.

INDIVIDUALS AND THEIR MOTIVATION

"We begin with what seems a paradox. The world of experience of any normal man is composed of a tremendous array of discriminably different objects, events, people, impressions . . . But were we to utilize fully our capacity for registering the differences in things and to respond to each event encountered as unique, we would soon be overwhelmed by the complexity of our environment . . . The resolution of this seeming paradox . . . is achieved by man's capacity to categorize. To categorize is to render discriminably different things equivalent, to group objects and events and people around us into classes . . . The process of categorizing involves . . . an act of invention . . . If we have learned the class "house" as a concept, new exemplars can be readily recognized. The category becomes a tool for further use. The learning and utilization of categories represents one of the most elementary and general forms of cognition by which man adjusts to his environment."[13]

NEEDS AND EXPECTATIONS

All individuals have needs and expectations. Some of those needs and expectations are provided by compensation, by the work environment and their leaders, and some provided by family and friends. As leaders we must understand and accept these needs. The informed leader not only understand the tasks assigned his followers, but in a much deeper sense he understands the individual followers and their own set of very unique needs and expectations. When individuals act in accordance with these needs and expectations, they act from motivations defined as either extrinsic or intrinsic.

EXTRINSIC MOTIVATION

Extrinsic motivation comes not from the task in progress, but from money or reward for doing the task. The task itself may be unpleasant, but the compensation may offer enough motivation for its completion.

INTRINSIC MOTIVATION

Intrinsic motivation occurs because the individual enjoys the task. He may enjoy it because of its challenge, he may enjoy it because of his sense of satisfaction, but he basically finds the task itself satisfying. Leaders have roles in addressing both types of motivation and will often combine each of these types of motivation in seeking the personal development of followers. Creating a positive and fulfilling work environment with a cohesive team for example, will enhance intrinsic motivation.

BEHAVIOR AND GOALS

Individual behavior results in the constant assessment and reassessment of goals. We set goals, assess and modify goals as our lives change. It is a constant process that ranges from what we decide to do today to what we hope to achieve by the year's end. We may set goals based on extrinsic or intrinsic motivation. Leaders may set goals for themselves and similar reasons, but they also are involved in setting goals for individual members as well as the group they lead. This is a vital part of the leader's role in the personal development of followers.

Goals are typically expressed clearly, or should be, in organizations. But the goals of individuals are seldom clear cut to the leader. Leaders then, must understand their people well enough to assist them in goal setting in the organizational environment. Choosing the right people is a part of the transactional paradigm, but motivating and encouraging people is a fundamental part of the transformational. As leaders the goals we set for ourselves and our followers have certain requirements. Prior to starting out in the process of goal setting, we should ask the following questions.

- **Are the goals something which can be measured readily?**
- **Are they specific and clearly stated?**
- **Am I prepared and willing to review and monitor these goals with the members of my group and devote the time required to the effort?**
- **Am I willing to do this in a participative process, with the members of the group involved in open discussion?**
- **Do we have the resources to support the task completion?**

The leader who is able to answer all of these questions positively is ready to begin the process. The development of goals that are clear, concise, and measurable is an important part of the process. One of the primary reasons for setting goals is to direct the attention of the group to areas of interest which pertain to the group. Another is to concentrate and focus the resources of the group on those areas. Often the resources of the group are not fully recognized until a formal goal setting process is initiated. It is the responsibility of the leader to the greater organization and to his group to be aware of all the resources available to him in the talents of his followers.

FIGURE 5

"People are all the same. They are all different"

ZENO

Thoughtful   steady   disciplined   loyal   dependable
funny   intelligent   expressive
amiable   outgoing   thorough   articulate
   Persistent   reliable   nervous   calm
   Creative   sincere   analytical   punctual   difficult
funny   withdrawn

The qualities of the individual are many, and there are few job descriptions that are a perfect fit. It's the job of the leader to decide which elements of the job description are absolute, and must be met. Leaders must understand this. They must also understand that often, the job description must be reshaped to match the person. Leaders are challenged with the task of knowing their people and the tasks they pursue in detail. As leaders gain knowledge of the capabilities of their people, they must also be attentive to the weaknesses of their followers. It is in addressing these capabilities and weaknesses that leaders often find the greatest fulfillment of their roles. Development of people is an abiding interest of the true leader.

FEEDBACK

Giving feedback to goal seekers is not mere criticism or simple benchmarking of their progress. It should involve the sincere attempt to support the efforts of the individual. True leaders care greatly for the development of their people and actively work with followers to achieve goals together.

OBJECTIVES

THE DESIRED OUTCOMES OF LEADERSHIP STUDY

- To provide a structural framework for the study and implementation of leadership
- To understand the nature of leadership as a *human* oriented effort
- To understand the importance of motivating collectively and individually throughout the organization
- To be able to distinguish the differences and potential for leadership versus traditional management
- To realize the amplifying nature of properly applied leadership to the bottom line of the company
- To understand through historical and contemporary evidence, the unchanging nature of leadership and human nature
- To understand through historical and contemporary evidence the nature of rapid and often chaotic change and how to offset this change with human capital.
- To gain a basic knowledge of the individual, the group, and the larger organization and apply these concepts to the particular situation of the reader
- To be able to realize the value of a potential "leadership moment" as revealed in the various case studies and seize and implement that opportunity.
- To foster a knowledge in the reader to learn continuously the concepts of leadership
- To understand the importance and nature of organizational culture and its impact on leaders and followers

- ○ To enable the new or emerging leader with the tools to motivate and develop followers in a positive and ethical manner
- ○ to be able to evaluate and assess the new group and to develop a vision for its success

It has been said that leadership cannot be taught but can be learned. If that is correct, and possible, then the objective of this material is to provide significant and sufficient learning experiences for the reader. Most business case studies concentrate on high level issues like strategy. The pedagogy of leadership learning has been attempted many times and in many forms and has proven a difficult challenge to many writers. In this effort we will reconstruct events in a format that will provide a vicarious experience of leadership. In short, we attempt to provide a leadership experience to you, the reader, and allow you to experience that event. Some of these were personal experiences, and some were leadership experiences told by others. The common denominator is that they were all real events. None are hypothetical or theoretical. It is hoped that in revealing how various leaders have applied leadership in critical instances, the reader will grasp the potential for application in their own circumstances.

The cases are more interesting to approach in this manner because they represent visible and clear "leadership moments" used by many people in a variety of situations. One of the primary factors in becoming an effective leader is to know when such a leadership moment occurs, and to act on that opportunity. Often such a moment may come in crisis, but many are routine events that occur daily in a number of situations.

In applying these cases we can be guided by the U.S. Military Academy leadership ethic of "Be, Know, And Do".[14] Successful leaders must be someone trusted by their followers. They must in turn know their followers and themselves, and finally they must be prepared to *act* in situations that further their vision and that of their followers in a positive and ethical manner. The military emphasis on leadership stems from one single fact. Leaders in the military environment train to deal with life and death decisions. Leadership is not an incidental study in the military. It is central to the military profession and the military way of life. We will introduce the military model and use several cases to illustrate how the military approaches leadership.

There are moments which must be seized by action if leadership is to flourish. Sometimes, if these moments are neglected, a leader loses such a great deal of credibility that he cannot recover. One of the goals of the aspiring leader is to know when those moments emerge, and to take advantage of them. By presenting the leadership moments of real-life leaders in such moments, it is hoped that the reader will understand how these moments transition from ideas to action, and in this manner be able to recognize those situations and act on them.

It is also important to understand the basic theories of the organization and the group within it, and the psychology of the individual. No leader exists without influence from his group and the larger organization, and no successful leader becomes so without knowledge of the unlimited variables of human personality. No leader can influence the group and greater organization without knowledge of their basic dynamics.

The reader will also be exposed to a number of the forms and faces of leadership employed by a cross section of leaders both historically well known and others. These are the descriptive terms of the actions carried out by successful leaders. They may be discussed as persuasion, indulgence, confidence, or a host of other terms, but they always imply action. They are the "do" of the "be, know, and do".

Structure can be an essential element if used properly. It can be a destructive element if used otherwise. We will present examples of both situations. Accountability is a key factor facing many institutions. While there is often sufficient accountability for the financial elements (often, not always) there is typically insufficient accountability regarding elements that improve the quality of leadership. An awareness of these elements and how they can be improved with accountability, structure, and metrics is desirable.

Very few individuals plan to be leaders, or enter a position of leadership with a vision and leader plan in mind. This is especially true of people in their first leadership position, and less so of leaders at the top of organizations. But it is essential that new leaders understand the reality that shapes leadership roles. These roles are sometimes defined by the larger organization and the constraints and culture it imposes. Finding a path to working with these factors can sometimes make or break the new leader.

Superimposed over all of these individual issues and tools of leadership is the idea of a philosophy of leadership. This philosophy is the driving element of leaders. All of the individual issues become meaningless unless we seek to develop a philosophy of leadership. That philosophy once formed becomes the essence of how we choose to work with people and treat them.

The human component is the most important of the three legs of the organizational stool. With too little attention to this component, even the best organized and most efficient quantitative systems can fail. With the motivation of its people, an organization can often overcome deficiencies in other areas. Effective leaders understand the importance of people to the organization. This goes beyond the transactional and simply knowing that employee "A" has to be at work between hours 8-5 to perform task "X". The Christian gospel admonishes the reader that "man cannot live by bread alone".[15] The effective leader understands this, albeit in a somewhat different context, and addresses the spiritual component of work. The spiritual component takes the leader beyond the transactional to greater possibilities for human accomplishment by appealing to the potential of the follower. When this potential is reached, the barriers to achievement are shattered. Leadership works best as a change agent when it lifts the spirit of the individual.

We will address the similarities and differences between the traditional management system and the system of transformational leadership in later chapters in greater detail, but the leader must understand the nature of each of these systems and how each is different but requires the other for a complete approach to leadership. It has been my experience that new and emerging leaders may often tend to focus on the traditional management model to the exclusion of the leadership paradigm. Neither model should be exclusive to the other. To lead in the fullest sense, the leader must embrace both of these and utilize them in a dynamically changing role as challenges dictate. There are situations that call for a nearly complete application of the transactional model, while others move closer to the end of the transformational spectrum. Knowing how to balance the uses of each of these can be very difficult, but very effective when applied properly.

Leaders typically work within two organizational structures. The working group which they lead may be the same as the larger organization, but most often leaders, especially the first-time leader, will have responsibility for a smaller group within the larger entity.

We live during a time of rapid and dynamic change. We are often told that we must change the manner in which we relate to people to accommodate the external change undergone by organizations. It is true that the precision and accuracy of measurements have developed to unforeseen levels. These levels do require greater precision and accuracy for certain tasks, but the essential nature of the human spirit has not changed. The qualities of a good leader, such as Alexander the Great, are essentially the same as they were in the time of Alexander. The external environment has changed and the forces acting on the organization are different, but those who occupy the places in the organizations internal components are no different. Understanding the timelessness of human nature, and accepting the challenge of working in a continually changing external environment should be objectives for good leaders.

THE MILITARY MODEL

We briefly introduced the transactional model earlier. We'll investigate it a bit further in this chapter as we take a look at the military model and try to understand why it performs as it does. You recall that we said that the transactional model and its companion, the transforming model, must exist together. The military is perhaps the best example of that requirement for mutual existence. There are few places if any, in the modern business establishments, where such a system of procedures, controls, hierarchies, and strict transactional models exist as in the military. There are also few examples of selfless dedication, service, and deeds of exemplary nature that exist outside of the military. Why this paradox?

The Western military model has its origins in the Roman Army.[16] In fact, the military model of the Roman Army is the predecessor of the modern corporation. Long before corporations existed, the Roman Army developed systems of hierarchy, divisions of labor, and functional departments. The success of the Roman Army enabled the success of the Roman Empire, not only militarily but also because the military organization was mirrored in the public administration of the Empire.

The military typically begins its work with the basic raw material, a young, fit, and impressionable teenager. For the most part, there is no comparison to the hiring process in civilian institutions. You take what is sent, although there is a process of attrition at certain phases. The indoctrination is rigorous. Expectations are set and accountability is defined. The consequences of both positive and negative behaviors are clearly articulated. Limits and boundaries are known. The history of the organization and its traditions are presented. Rites of passage are carried out at major steps in one's career. Promotions and pay come at certain specific times, and those times vary only in rare exceptions, based only on unusual merit. No member has a "better deal" and the pay of all is publicly known. Physical fitness is required and frequently tested. The value system and examples of military virtues and excellence in each service are described as history, and the hope that the new recruit will find in himself the capacity to carry on that history is issued as a challenge. Accountability is required of all and at every level, and discipline is enforced. Frequent personnel evaluations are conducted at specific intervals and boards meet with regularity to decide on promotions. The enterprise covers the entire globe. Despite all of this structure, the military still possesses the ability to display remarkable flexibility. Who can forget the small footprint of Afghanistan, with U.S. Special Operations troops riding the backs of horses as they sought out the Taliban? Despite the hierarchical organization, the military knows when to organize differently for results. This is a tremendous task. Imagine that the 18 year-old sailor will in one year from now be standing watch in the reactor compartment of a nuclear submarine. Think of the infantry private who may be a squad leader, on patrol in the streets of Iraq next year, or the airman who will operate the boom on a refueling tanker, or a lieutenant in charge of a platoon. In all the preparation for these tasks, the transactional model is the starting point. But superimposed over all of this task-related preparation is an ethos of leadership and character. The organization's values and culture are driven home with clarity. Teamwork is paramount. The group's hardships are shared by all of its members. Every General has at some time in their career, slept on the ground. Captains of Navy Ships have stood watches at sea and been department heads, and

Battalion Commanders have led platoons. The progression upward is regulated and monitored, and only those who have been through a succession of increasing responsibilities and challenges are considered for promotion. Trust is considered one of the greatest values in both leaders and their subordinates. No one rises to the top of the military structure without experiencing all of the steps expected of them along the route.

In examining the military model, it's useful to think of the scope and breadth of the military and its operations. The military works in air, land, and on and below the sea. The US Army alone had active duty personnel strength of more than 500,000 in 2008. The Navy and Air Force each possess about 320,000 and the Marines approach 200,000, and none of these numbers include the strength levels of reserve forces. Only Exxon Mobil and Wal-Mart, each with about 200,000 employees and numerous operating sites approach the smallest military organization. With these large numbers of people and scattered, sometimes remote operating sites, it should be clear that structure and excellent communications play a large role in day-to-day operations. Rules, procedures, clear lines of communication, command and control are absolutely necessary. Add to this the fact that the cultures of the various branches of the US military have been in existence with minor changes for more than 200 years, and you have an enormous legacy of leadership history from which to learn.

At the heart of the operations order in a military unit is a tacit transactional understanding; "you will". It is this clear understanding that forms the basis for a transformational opportunity in a business or a military operation. It's probably an irony to some that the institution that is credited with the most selfless displays of transformational leadership has at its core a hard-nosed transactional exchange. Failure is not acceptable. Lives depend on success and the execution of orders. You will and you must. The performance of a sustained transactional system is what enables leadership to thrive. Without this, you cannot begin the transformation of a culture or allow leadership to take root.

Most corporations of a certain size have policies and procedures. That's a start. But having policies and procedures is useless unless there are systems of accountability and the willingness and discipline to enforce them. If they are enforced, it must be done with predictability and accountability, and above all fairness. It's also worth noting that there are times when a heightened awareness of regulations serves the corporation better. If you are assuming a position in a company with an objective of building a safety culture, and regulations regarding safety have been disregarded, then safety regulations deserve close scrutiny. Without the possibility of sanctions for the violation of policy, regulations and policy have no useful existence. This is a simple statement regarding a simple rule, but the consequences for ignoring the basics in this can be serious. Without the expectation of a sanction, and in the face of repeated violations, the integrity of management comes into dispute. Once that happens a cascade of mistrust flows throughout the organization, and it takes serious effort to restore trust.

In modern corporations, the lack of accountability is probably the factor most responsible for the failure to reach objectives. It is most often not the very sophisticated techniques which are ignored, but rather the most basic. Discipline, the characteristic of faithfully following the policies and procedures laid down by leadership, enables and supports accountability. Without those two, goals become difficult if not impossible.

LEADERSHIP CAPITAL

To become a true leader, and not just an organizationally appointed supervisor, you have to earn the trust, confidence, and respect of your subordinates. To do that requires leadership capital. It's a capital expense of a different kind, and most new managers and supervisors have never been exposed to its qualities. It calls for an investment on your part, and leaders spend it wisely but frequently. Leadership capital can take many forms. It can be as simple as spending time with the people for whom you are responsible. It sometimes requires that the leader see an opportunity for a "leadership moment", and seizes the opportunity skillfully. At the core of the concept of leadership capital is the realization that it is people who drive events in the organization.

There are a number of general concepts that most of the people who write about leadership agree on;

- ○ Leadership is a process involving people
- ○ Leadership is a quality that motivates people to deliver beyond the transactional contract
- ○ Leadership transforms the people and the workplace
- ○ Leadership is difficult to define but is recognized when it is seen
- ○ Leadership involves a process between follower and leader that is influential
- ○ Leadership depends heavily on interpersonal communication
- ○ Leaders and followers both have roles in the process

Perhaps the most important aspect of military leadership is the objective of creating an individual who is self-motivated and team oriented. Individuals who are brilliant but isolated contributors seldom rise to prominence in the military. One exception might be intelligence analysts, but even in this capacity it is necessary to work with others, often to persuade them of your discoveries. Having the emotional capacity to place the team above self is a key indicator of success in the military environment.

With these general ideas, it is still challenging to characterize leadership. Over many years of work in the military and the civilian world, I found it possible to use the lessons of certain events as indicators of leadership. Some of these events were extremely important, with lives in the balance or investments at risk. Sometimes, they were simple events that might go unnoticed or certainly never be seen as important. But in all of these, there were hints that leadership was taking place.

MANAGING ENTRY INTO THE ORGANIZATION—(SOCIALIZATION)

How you conduct the entry of a new employee into your organization is very important, and can have far reaching consequences. In an earlier chapter we talked about how a military organization goes about managing the process of joining. The whole process is perhaps the most closely managed event in that person's life and one of the most closely managed and controlled events in the military. Why so much attention to this? As with most things in organizations, we must always look to the transactional model and its requirements. With military recruits, we are asking them to embrace a completely new and alien culture with rigid transactional foundations. We do this because we have every intention of transforming them into that culture as compliant members within a very short time frame. It works very well, so well that the times for doing this and the expectations have changed little over decades. That first part is only the beginning. With the technology needed to bring a large force into leading edges of battle technologies, we cannot begin the advanced task and technical training until we are sure that the new recruit understands the culture, social conventions, and regulations of their service.

In the Israeli Defense Force, for example, a great deal of importance is attached to the entry of a recruit into the Force. In certain units of the IDF, the swearing in ceremony is conducted at the scene of great victories earned in the 1948 and 1967 wars. In most of the Western world, soldiers are administered an oath of office that dates back to Roman times when the oath was called the *sacramentum*. [17]

One of the essential elements of managing entry is to go past the transactional and establish a sense of belonging and purpose to the new employee. If you work for a large organization, the chances are that parts of this role belong to the Human Resources department. But parts only. The HR department will concern itself with personnel policy, legal and benefits issues. These are largely administrative, but the responsibility of making the new recruit familiar with the specifics of the job, and introducing them to the group in which they will be working cannot be delegated. It is the first important task of the leader with regard to the new team member.

One of the desired outcomes to managing entry is to instill in the new member a sense of belonging to a group that places a value on them. The other is to acquaint them with the job and communicate the expectations of the company. It's at this point that you need to ask questions.

The time used in managing entry has another advantage. You have the opportunity to view the new employee before the pressures of the job begin to come down on either of you. Using this time well often gives you a view of the person that would not have developed during the typical interview. It's also a chance to spend wisely on leadership capital. His perception of his value to the organization is proportional to the time you spend on getting him ready for the work. Let's revisit the military model. We talked of how the services teach their history and culture, and deliver the expectations of the institution that the new recruit will perpetuate the service's values in their career. There are clear expectations. It's one reason why the Navy can take an 18-year-old and send him to nuclear reactor training so that when he reports to his first duty station, the Commanding Officer has a very good idea of what he is getting and how they will perform. Standards, processes and procedures are drilled and drilled again until they become almost automatic. The process of joining is augmented well by systems and procedures. In this manner, the task environment is given a jump-start, usually by a training facility. This means that the field leader receives a new member to which he can attribute some quality of training. This does not, of course, absolve the field leader from delivery of additional training. In a recent training program instituted for commercial truck drivers, we made a point of spending time with them before they departed for their area offices and new jobs at the conclusion of their training. We asked them what about the seven days of training impressed them most. This company had never invested in driver training before, and the answers were clear. Most every driver noted that he was impressed that we spent the time and money on them, and that their own feelings of self-worth were increased as a result. Some had never experienced an airplane flight before. Contrast this with the easy-come and easy-go attitude of some employers, and you begin to see the importance of managing the joining process. Training may be ultimately be done by another person or department within your organization. However, if you are the manager of people, you have as a primary responsibility to understand the task and the readiness of your team to perform it. It's a big part of accepting the responsibility that comes with managing people. Even if you will never have to perform the task yourself, such as the infantry officer or sergeant who must be proficient with all the tasks of his team, you still have the obligation to support them. This includes your support in making certain that they are trained in all respects to perform the task. Clearly, if you are going to provide support, you must have more than a passing acquaintance of the task, and you must also have the ability to discern their performance against some objective scale. How do we go about doing that?

Here is a sample analysis approach. You can tailor this to the specific roles within your group.

1. **JOB FUNCTIONS**—Describe these at a very high level. List as many functions as seem to be required by the job, then describe each of the functions in detail.

2. **CRITICAL TASKS**—Within the functions, there will be some that are critical to the success of the function. Justify why they are critical to the function and then rank in order of importance.

3. **COMPONENT TASKS**—Each of the critical tasks should have a component task, or sub-task. These compose the larger tasks. Describe them.

4. **TASK FREQUENCY OR REPETITION**—How often does this task repeat? Identify a standard for completion and frequency. Do this for both critical and component tasks. Is the standard reasonable? What support is necessary for you, as a leader, to deliver to your team?

5. **ACCEPTABLE ERROR**—What is the acceptable level of performance for this group of tasks? Define this clearly, as it will become your quality standard. Do this for both critical and component tasks.

6. **WORK CONDITIONS**—See for yourself what the work conditions are. Look at noise, lighting, temperature, safety, distractions, and any other issues that may affect performance. As a leader, this is one of your most critical responsibilities. It is one that when done properly, and for the support of your team, will bring you enormous respect and good will.

7. **SKILL REQUIREMENTS**—What are the minimum requirements for a new worker in this job? Are they properly observed?

8. **KEY PERFORMANCE INDICATORS OR PRODUCTION UNITS**—What are the production units of the task when delivered properly? Define them by specific units of measurement, e.g. Tons per day, circuit boards per hour, miles driven, etc. What are the consequences of failure to deliver? What is your planned "work-around" if you experience equipment failure, personnel loss, or other work stoppage?

This process works in both directions. As you acquire new team members, you should have this process in place for each of the job functions. And conversely, as you assume new roles the same set of process standards can be used to evaluate your entry into a new position. Simply by going through this structured process, you will gain an understanding of each of the jobs of your team, even if you have no prior experience. In large and well—established companies, especially those with a production management environment, these factors are usually already established. Often you may have access to statistics or historical performance data. But you must still take the responsibility for assuring the continuation of processes already in place. The steps described above work toward the fulfillment of the transactional model. As we work to improve them with our teams in a leader's role, we begin to fulfill the transformational model. Transforming leaders will not hesitate to get on the factory floors, ride in the cabs of trucks, or work alongside their teams on assembly lines in order to grasp the challenges of the job. When they do this, they spend, and earn, valuable leadership capital and gain the respect of their teams.

Some final comments are essential to complete our understanding of the process of joining the organization. In the section immediately preceding, we outlined the transactional elements of the work for the new team member. What are the "softer" elements? What are the outcomes that will support and drive a transformational culture? In the simplest and most concise terms, we seek to create a sense of belonging and mission. You are one of us, this is what we do, and this is how we do it. The sense of belonging is a powerful motivational element. When this occurs, some really great things can happen within an organization. Successful families share the same traits. We have histories and hopeful futures. We have traditions and rules. We're not talking about the extremes of some of the movements that swept the management culture in the 1970's like nap rooms and sensitivity sessions. There's no need for a permissive culture. Nurturing combined with discipline is a better method. If the new employee emerges from the process of joining with a sense of belonging and mission, you are off to a good start. To do this, someone in the organization has to spend leadership capital, and commit to its ongoing use in the future. A successful joining process must be continued and supplemented or its usefulness ends when the process is over. It has to be a continually evolving system, tuned and improved over time.

SUMMARY OF THE MILITARY MODEL

- Being, knowing, and doing as a leader
- Shared Difficulties
- Presence at crisis
- Structured career paths and subordinate development
- Predictable sanctions, positive and negative
- Discipline and Accountability
- Unit history and challenges to excellence
- The crucible of combat and its effects

THE CONSTANT LEADER

We know that change is not only inevitable, but now occurs more rapidly than ever before. Technology drives change, and technology is moving so quickly that even the most capable observers have trouble keeping up. Businesses are somewhat like teams of rafters or canoeists running rapids. One mistake in the rushing stream and everybody falls out. One of my favorite quotes is from one of the Greek philosophers, who noted, "You never step in the same river twice".[18] One modern writer challenged this by noting that you never step in the same river once.

The step itself constitutes a change to the river. The mission of organizations change, the structure changes, they come and go. Products reach obsolescence quickly. The nature of employment itself is changing, with people making more frequent moves. What is there that does not change?

One thing that has not changed in significant fashion is the principles of leadership. These principles work universally across cultures, languages, and institutions. Bad leadership looks the same in any setting. So does good leadership. If we go back to examine the open systems model, we see that the greatest influence comes from external sources. We have little control over those conditions. What we do have control over are the conditions under which we work with respect to each other. Transformational leaders understand their role in this scenario. They are able to embrace and challenge external chaos by providing a calm and stable internal environment. True leaders work toward establishing that environment in many ways. One view that most followers have of a true leader is usually that they see them as predictable. The followers have embraced the vision of the leader, which is also constant and predictable. The emotional equilibrium of the leader generates an emotional equilibrium in the group. It becomes a safe, positive place where everyone understands the task and the motives. This kind of atmosphere can only increase productivity and morale.

One of my favorite movie scenes is from "Patton", when actor George C. Scott's character is told by one of his aides that he does not know when the General is acting and when he is serious. Scott replies that it is not important that anyone else needs to know, it's only necessary for him. The really great military leaders will sometimes admit that there is a certain demeanor that is sometimes compared with acting. But whatever you decide to call it, the most important thing is to never let your fears be known in a crisis. Passion and intensity are fine if they are needed, but once you begin to show fear in a crisis, the entire team takes on that fear. Confidence is contagious. So are fear, doubt, and a host of other negative attitudes. That does not mean that you cannot be honest. But honesty and panic do not work well together.

In these first few paragraphs we have talked about crisis and the role of the leader in such events. Hopefully, you will not face that level of crises very often. The second level of the constant leader has to do with things that are much simpler, but still important. We are talking now of rules, processes, procedures. These are the structural things that make your role as a leader more predictable and the outcomes and expectations more predictable too. One of the questions asked of military personnel is "what if . . . ?" Aboard ship, Captains routinely ask watch teams, "What do you do if this happens?" They expect, and usually get, the response desired. There are two reasons for this. The first is that the drills usually are done in anticipation of the things that most commonly occur. The other is that the teams are asked to be thinking constantly of what might occur, even if there is no drill for it.

FAIRNESS AND CONSTANCY

As a small group leader, one of the most damaging things you can do is to fail to sanction even-handedly. By sanction we mean the distribution of positive and negative actions regarding subordinates. There is an old Navy rule that applies. "Praise in public, rebuke in private." It's a good rule and useful in most every circumstance I can think of. This does not mean that you cannot bring a violation of a procedure to the attention of a subordinate immediately, such as a safety or health issue. What it does mean is that once that is done, the administration of any sanction should take place privately. Humiliation is not a morale builder in the workplace. Good leaders bring emotional equilibrium to the workplace. In praising or reprimanding, they are even—tempered and thoughtful.

REACHING EMOTIONAL EQUILIBRIUM

It is often the action of the leader when confronted with a crisis that forms the most enduring image in the eyes of his followers. What might be some of the methods that help the leader build that ability and equilibrium? One of the tasks facing you as you assume your first leadership role is that of knowing the work at hand. What do your people do? Here, we fall back again to the transactional model. What is the contract or agreement that they have been paid to do? What is its scope and depth? If you do not know that, you have failed in the most basic way. Note that we say that you must know what they are paid to do. You need not be able to do it yourself, though in some cases and some work environments that is an additional requirement or certainly an additional value. In the US Submarine Service, officers and enlisted perform similar tasks and in many cases it is an enlisted sailor who will sign off on a section of the officers qualification record. This is because the tasks are almost all critical and their incorrect application will mean danger to the crew. Thus it happens that in gaining the approval of an enlisted sailor regarding a task, an officer may also gain their trust. Trust and confidence are inextricably linked in this kind of environment. Each of these attributes contributes to the overall equilibrium of the group. While this is not applicable to every situation in the civilian sector, it is a valuable thing to do. If you truly want to learn of the difficulties of a task, try doing it for a while. Have one of your people instruct you. You will have gained their respect by doing so. You also fulfill elements of the transactional model by gaining firsthand knowledge of the work. You cannot effectively supervise, mentor, or sanction someone who works as a subordinate without having a secure grasp of the work they are doing. Subordinates will form their opinion of you by their judgment of your competence. Competence will generate confidence, and in turn trust. These things all contribute to the emotional equilibrium of the workplace.

There may be some question as to how far should you go in becoming competent. Since your task is to lead, then doesn't your becoming fully competent in the task of a subordinate simply create another worker, and not a leader? We will most often see this problem with someone who is promoted from the task position of a subordinate to a leader role. Often, they wish to retain their competence in the former role and they move back and forth into the position as needs dictate. The answer to the question is that it depends on the circumstances. In the Army or Marine Corps, especially in the small unit leadership ranks that are composed of Sergeants through Captains, competence tends to be something needed throughout the leadership. Everyone must fight. The survival of the group depends on it. Infantry privates will not follow a sergeant or lieutenant who does not know how to fire and maintain a weapon. The role of competence of leaders in civilian institutions is a bit harder to define, but it can be done. As a general rule, the greater the technical content of the task, the greater the need for competence of a leader at the small group level. Indeed, the vetting process for many promotions calls for specific and detailed experience in the fields in which the leader will supervise.

LEADING CULTURAL CHANGE

Over the years and as an MBA student, corporate trainer, project manager and military officer, I have read countless books and articles on leadership. As I went over many of those articles and books in preparation for writing this book, I discovered a very practical and workable premise by Edgar Schein, an MIT professor and psychologist who specializes in organizational culture and leadership. [19] In a chapter titled "How Leaders Embed and Transmit Culture," Schein describes ten mechanisms by which leaders change corporate cultures through visible actions. As I reviewed these actions, I tried to recall from personal experience and from my reading of military history how these actions would fit my real world experiences. Much of the leadership literature is theoretical and describes traits not easily observable or difficult to put into practice. The Schein model offers the most practical set of guidelines for aspiring leaders, and also offers an audit tool for critical analysis of leaders' actions. It's also an attractive model in the manner in which he describes leadership as a cultural change agent. As I read through his description of change leaders, I came to the understanding that he tried less to describe the necessary traits of a leader than he did to prescribe actions of a leader. When viewed against the overwhelming numbers of theoretical essays on leadership, his model seems eminently workable. By defining leaders as those who act in a particular manner, he allows us to focus on the context of the action. He separates the actions into five primary and five secondary mechanisms of cultural change. It's important for us as leaders to understand that in our roles, we are attempting cultural change. We move along the spectrum of transactional toward transformational, balancing the needs of the group and the larger organization. We must understand that any movement along the spectrum of change away from the pure transactional points toward transformational. Unless you have entered into a perfect world of a new leader in an already transformed environment, you have the task of cultural change, even if it is at the small group level only.

The primary (direct) mechanisms are:

> Focus or Attention
> Crisis Response
> Role Modeling
> Sanctions
> Criteria for selection and dismissal

The secondary (indirect) mechanisms are:

> Design of organizational structure
> Design of systems and procedures
> Design of facilities
> Stories, legends, and myths
> Formal mission statements

PRIMARY MECHANISMS

Notice that the first groups of actions are directed toward people, while the secondary mechanisms are all about systems, processes, rules and regulations.

Attention—In their communication of corporate vision, core values, and other issues, we can discern what our leaders believe to be important to them, and consequently, what they believe should be important to us. This is the method by which we become acquainted with their value system. It is the intent of the leader that followers internalize these values, and leaders ensure that this occurs in many ways, but the most frequent method is through their verbal and written statements. Military missions and operations orders are very strongly oriented to specific objectives and attention/focus. Operations orders and mission briefings in the military are heavy on the use of verbs such as "you will . . ." This is their method of ensuring attention, and it's done with timetables, milestones, and other discrete tools of the transactional.

Crisis Response—Among historical examples of the actions of well-known military leaders this action is probably one of the most frequently cited. During the crucible of combat, emotions are heightened dramatically. The true military leader understands the nature of combat and the necessity of responding in a manner that will motivate his teams. This method is displayed by action of the leader. Crisis response is something that must always be attended by a strong focus on the part of the leader. If leaders truly have the best interests of the team as part of their focus, they will almost certainly react properly in times of crisis. If a leader fails to respond in the interests of his team during a crisis, the heightened emotions of the moment typically generate a strong negative perception of the values of the leader. In most civilian institutions, we see less opportunity for crisis response than in the military, especially during combat. But there are opportunities for leadership capital to be spent in crisis situations, even in civilian organizations. It cannot be emphasized strongly enough the loss of confidence that leaders subject themselves to in failing to respond to a moment of crisis. The perception is simple and straightforward. You are seen as not caring. If there is any time and place in your tenure as a leader where you absolutely must be present, it is during a crisis. Once you fail to appear, you have lost a tremendous opportunity to spend leadership capital. You will usually be unable to retrieve it. Distancing yourself from the crisis also places psychological distance between you and your team. Think of the crisis response as a test of attention and focus. If you fail to support your team by your participation and presence when necessary, it shows a lack of attention to the team. I see this as a sort of behavioral version of the Miranda warning given by police. Whatever you say or fail to say, do or fail to do, will be used against you in the corporate court of opinion. Your downward loyalty is being tested in this kind of event. The key operating principle here is that while you cannot control the timing of external events such as accidents, financial problems, and other issues, you can and must control the response of your teams to these events. For this you will be recognized as a leader.

Managers will attempt to plan their way through a crisis. This is good, as we have noted that we always seek a balance between the transactional and transformational. They will put in place the various procedures and controls that allow the crisis to be contained at least to some degree by their management actions. These procedures and controls are necessary and valuable. But it will almost always be the response of the leader in the situation that will be most remembered by their followers. This is especially true when the actions of the leader supports and enhances the actions of their followers. Controls and procedures channel the responses of the organization and its people in a predictable manner and lend some order to chaos by mandating a set of responses, but they need to be attended by the presence and caring attitudes of a leader.

There is another valuable component of crisis management that gives leaders an advantage when responding to a crisis. This comes when the leader has instituted a set of controls that gives a warning that a crisis is about to develop. These controls act as a type of early warning indicator, and will allow the manager and leader to focus on the content of the response to the crisis.

It's important for us to realize a distinction that occurs when trying to assess crisis responses. In many of the military situations of crisis, there is a time-critical factor. By that we mean that something has to be done immediately, with little opportunity for analysis. For that reason the military often emphasizes their small group leaders and immediately higher ranks to consider possible scenarios and have a planned response. Sometimes you can plan, sometimes you cannot, and sometimes an event occurs that no one could have foreseen. If you miss the opportunity to provide support and leadership capital in a crisis, you may still have a chance to regain trust.

How can this be done? If the omission is obvious, and you have made an error, the best chance you have to regain the trust of your team is to acknowledge your mistake. Leaders are far from infallible, but they are respected most when they show their fallibility and honesty. It's called humility. It is one of the qualities that creates followers and is an indication of the authentic leader.

Role Models—Focal leaders, those appointed by the organization, represent the authority of the organization. If the stated objectives and values of leaders conflict with their behavior, their followers accept the values of the action as true. Practice what you preach is the primary rule for leaders. This principle also applies to situations where the transactional model is violated, thus generating dissonance among followers and confusion over procedures and policies. The typically accepted term for this situation is cognitive dissonance. It is rare in the military for a sergeant or Captain not to have acknowledged the presence of a role model in their early careers, and typically their actions tend to follow closely what they viewed in their role model.

Sanctions—Sanctions are simply rewards and penalties. This is an element of the transactional that can have dramatic effects on the team, and serve to either support or detract from the leaders attempt at transformational leadership. It is critical that leaders understand the importance of administering sanctions through policy and personal actions in a fair and impartial manner.

Schein's model describes the use of rewards as having two objectives. These are the desired behavior, and the desired result.

An example of the importance of this might be the formulation of policy designed to improve safety through a series of prescribed actions. If a member has an improved safety record but has not applied any of the actions, there is a lack of cultural change on the part of that team member. If you reward that member for "luck" the result disrupts cohesion of the team and does not advance the objective of culture change. It's not just the results you are interested in, but the behavioral adjustment too.

Personnel Criteria—The most severe sanction is to remove a team member. Conversely, one of the most important sanctions, or rewards, is to approve or recommend the hiring of a member. At face value, this is a transactional event. I am going to hire someone and pay them "X" for doing "A, B, C". If we intend to transform culture and lead, we need to look beyond the transactional. We must determine more than the new members ability to do "A, B, C" and look toward the culture we want to build or change as leaders. If our group is indeed cohesive and tight, we may discuss their personality and how we think others may accept them. At this point we depart the transactional model for more difficult territory. In short, we are not hiring them for their task completion capability, but for other skills and compatibilities that will interact with our group. We will discuss group cohesion later, but for now you should understand that cohesion in a group will significantly affect productivity, and it works in both directions, positively and negatively.

SECONDARY MECHANISMS

Facility Design

So you say you are not an architect! No problem. If and when you climb to a high leadership role, you can actually fulfill this role of design from the bottom up. But as a small group leader, you have a more immediate and simpler role. You should evaluate the working spaces of your people and make those small local changes as necessary. Often, the smallest of actions dedicated to the safety and comfort of your team can make a big impact. Are the areas clean? Are they lighted properly? Above all, are they safe? Evaluate the places your team works. Decide if you would be willing to work in them for a day, week, or longer. If not, make them so and accept the grateful thanks of your team. You should never make a decision on approval or disapproval of a request to modify a work environment without experiencing it yourself. Good things happen when you venture into the places where your people spend their day.

Formal Mission Statements

These are often more directed toward top leadership. But occasionally, it becomes necessary for you as a small group leader to define the mission of your group. This may be required if you undergo a larger reorganization at the highest levels. It may be necessary if you take in people from other groups as your role expands or contracts. In many organizations that grow by acquisition, roles change. Often there are gray areas between group responsibilities. As these develop, it's very important to stop, analyze who is doing what, and whether or not that task belongs within your group. Failure to do that causes problems and contributes to morale problems and if not addressed, sometimes generates task failures. It's very embarrassing to have to say, "Oh, I thought your guys were going to take care of XYZ". Developing a statement forces everyone to stop, look at the roles, and determine if the organization is best served by the roles your group is playing.

Organizational Folklore and Tradition

The folklore of your organization consists of the verbal history of events that are reminiscent of its success, humorous events, and challenges met. It is more often referred to in terms of things such as sales victories or other corporate accomplishments that over time take on the shine of legends. In the military, this occupies a very strong place and is used often. The application of this is a good indicator of morale within the organization.

Organizational Structure

This can follow as a result of a mission statement as we discussed earlier, or be directed from the very top of the organization. But just like mission statements, it can also be appropriate to define structure at the lowest level of any organization. What we do as a group is one, and who does what within the group is the other. With a truly cohesive team in which each member knows the others well, sometimes the group assumes the role of supporting each other. When this occurs, productivity can soar. Often this will occur independently, without your direction. That's a good sign. If in selection of your team, you have formed a group with this tendency, you've done well. If you see this in action, your next task as a leader is to keep it in place, or sustain it. As people come and go, the group dynamics change, and it may be necessary to make structural changes to accommodate the changes in personnel. One of the most successful military adaptations of organizational structure is the composition and structure of Special Forces teams and other special operations groups in the military. Most often these teams are not led by the person senior in rank but rather with the requisite experience to bring about the result. This is a dramatic departure from the hierarchical structures of the past, but it has been proven many times, and most recently in Afghanistan. Often leadership presents as a paradox.

Policies, Procedures and Systems

As leaders of small groups and large, we have latitudes within our organizations. As you will see in another section, we sometimes have latitudes in deciding whether or not to use the policies and procedures to their fullest extent. As one of my great Commanding Officers once told me, "The book is what you use if you don't know what else to do". More than most institutions, the military has an abundance of these policies and procedures. They range from protocol for honors and ceremonies to the proper procedure for maintaining and firing a weapon. You may find that your civilian institution does not have adequate procedures. Or, as a new leader, you may believe that you have to use the book, rule, procedure, or policy in every applicable instance. There are occasions when that is so. Know what these are and reserve them for the most serious of situations. For example, in areas of external regulations such as Federal Agency requirements, a leader has no reason to circumvent the standing requirements. The same goes for safety and health. Use common sense in evaluating the situation and act accordingly. Know the difference between rules and guidelines. If you have sanctions in place for violations of a serious nature, you need to decide whether or not you are serious about following through on these. If you have a problem in retention of personnel, and you have a sanction that requires termination, you have to live with the result. Failure to terminate may cause a much greater problem than terminating the employee. This can result in loss of morale or the accusation that you are selectively enforcing company policies. Be sure that you have an understanding of the consequences of enforcing and not enforcing a rule, policy, or regulation. It takes courage in order to carry out decisions, especially when the consequences can impede progress. But without that courage, all the policies you develop are useless. The key point in assessing these things is to have a deliberate and thoughtful discussion about them. Pointless rules, policies and procedures are soon rendered useless, but the lack of them creates a completely separate class of problems. We have discussed briefly ten types of actions, the sum of which when imposed as a group, will enable leaders to effect cultural change. This sounds pretty simple right? Not quite. There is one overarching component missing from the previous discussion. It is called accountability. Without it, all of the work done toward establishing mechanisms of a transforming leader is without support.

Accountability—The Glue That Holds Things Together

Accountability ultimately depends upon sanctions for its application. Leaders who are not prepared or courageous enough to apply sanctions, positive or negative, will not become transformational or change cultures. Note how we have turned to the transactional model once more. This cycling back and forth is part of the balance that leaders need to establish cultural change. The actions that the Schein model proposes must be backed by sound accountability in the transactional mode. Accountability infers that something is being monitored and measured, and people will be responsible for failures. That is a basic trait of the transactional model, and it is basic to the success of organizations. One of the problems with establishing policies and procedures is monitoring them. In some cases, leaders are satisfied that things look good, and that's enough. Once the policy manuals are written and available for show-and-tell, their monitoring is neglected. Another problem is that somewhere down the line in the chain of command, a leader breaks the sequence and drops the ball. That's why systems must be developed that can be monitored and people made accountable. That's why systems must be developed that can be monitored and people made accountable. It takes discipline to execute and follow up.

As the Cold War between the US and Russia was winding down and relations were improving, the two nations agreed on arms reduction. One of the phrases to come out of the talks was "trust but verify". It's still not a bad slogan. I had a sort of classification that I used for deciding when I needed to verify. If the task was extremely critical and involved several people, I verified at several stages, but in an outwardly casual and uncritical manner. If I had a new team member, I verified. Once you have satisfied yourself that you know the task, and you know the people, you can make those decisions much more readily and with less stress. It's always important to remember that ultimately, you are the one accountable.

NARRATIVES AND CASES

The case study approach to leadership that we will use in this instance is based on the experiences of real life leaders as they responded to events in their respective careers. Cases have been selected from events in the military, business, and education arenas. Some are drawn from written history. It is intended that each of the cases will present participants and facilitators with a critical event which they will discuss and resolve as a group. The resolution of each case is presented as it occurred, but this should not prevent participants from developing alternative resolutions. It is in the discussion and facilitative process that true learning will develop. To that end, facilitators are encouraged to change the variables by addition or removal of context to stimulate a different response to the critical event, and thereby a different resolution. An example is to present the military cases, and then have participants compare and contrast the event as it would be resolved in a different type of organization. Most of the cases are brief, but properly applied they will generate extensive discussion and debate. Others are major cases that the original participants needed months to resolve. It should also be noted that there are very few "right" answers. In each of these cases, the original participants provided a resolution that for them seemed timely and correct. Leadership is not a science but a combination of art supported by science. The cases are intended to be used to generate discussion and debate and not didactic presentations. By combining groups of cases instead of generalizing from a single case, facilitators may make much better use of the exemplars in single case studies.

A central objective in these cases is to have the new leader understand the potential for a leadership moment in small and sometimes apparently insignificant events. Thus it is the *awareness* of the leader to view events, great and small, as potential opportunities to exercise leadership which transforms. Imagine that leaders have a rule which applies similarly to the portion of the Miranda warning which states that ". . . *anything you say can and will be used against you* . . ." Leaders are responsible for all things occurring within their area of responsibility. They are judged by their followers for both their actions and their utterances. The communication skills of leaders are the great enabler of leadership. What you communicate, how well or how badly you may communicate and the timing of your communications, all these things are important and contribute to a leader's ability to transform.

LEARNING OBJECTIVES FOR THE SECTION

- The general learning objectives for this section are:
- To gain a thorough understanding of some of the many transformative actions available to the leader
- To learn, in an experiential manner, how leaders have taken advantage of specific instances to develop followers
- When faced with the differences between the competing paradigms of transactional and transformational, to be able to establish the correct balance between the two

FACILITATIVE PROCESS METHODOLOGY

The cases presented are intended to be developed in a group facilitative environment and not a didactic presentation or lecture approach. For group facilitators unfamiliar with the approach, a much more detailed explanation can be found on the web at the site of the US Air Force Air War University.

www.au.af.mil/au/awc/awcgate/**sgitc**/reftoc.htm

The basic format consists of five sections. Each of these sections is presented in greater detail in the original document found above. They are very briefly presented here:

Preparation—to be completed by both facilitator and group. Facilitator should assign readings consistent with objectives to establish significant knowledge of foundational material, and especially the case to be discussed.

Introduction—The facilitator presents the case and context. Facilitators should feel free to change context, introduce other contextual factors, and modify and add questions to enhance the experience of discussion.

Interactive Dynamic Phase—The role of the facilitator is to generate discussion and creative conflict of ideas

Publishing and Processing—Findings, comments, and opinions are summarized and recorded.

Generalization and Conclusion—The facilitator observes and examines the group progress for the completion of learning objectives. This step will not be achieved unless a facilitator has a solid understanding of both the underlying principles of the behavioral traits of the individual and the group and is competent in applying the combination of these two traits in an experiential learning event.

MILITARY CASES

THE WEST POINT LEADER PLAN PROCESS

CASE OBJECTIVES

- ○ To acquaint the reader with a process plan to recognize, address, and act to resolve issues in leadership

CONTEXT

Take this bet . . .

I'll bet that 95 per cent of you have never have worked under a supervisor who discussed the term "leadership" in detail and assisted in developing a leader plan for you. The identification of root causes is critical to this process. I recall a discussion with a consultant who was working for our company. He told me that the company did a very good job of hiring smart and capable people, but that they never succeeded in developing systems to limit the root causes of their problems. Instead they used their capable employees to "put out fires" and thus kept having the same problems occurring over and over. He characterized it as the difference between putting out fires continuously and building a really good system to prevent fires. After a time, the culture begins to reward people for putting out fires, and neglects the causes of the fires. It's a colossal waste of talent, and since the organization never seems to learn, they are forced to solve the same problems over and over. Leaders act to institute beneficial change. Don't treat symptoms, treat the disease.

The West Point leadership training involves the adoption of a Leader Thought Process. At first glance, this seems very simple and straightforward. While it certainly may be that for many leadership issues, often issues will be much more complicated.

The leader thought process has three major areas.

- **What is happening?**
- **How do you account for what is happening?**
- **What actions are required of you as a leader?**

These three steps are a basis for the new leader. They represent the thought process required not only when entering a new leadership position, but as a constant process for leaders who occupy a position over a long term. In this brief introduction to leadership, we will deal only with the barest minimum of theories of leadership, of which there are many. The "What?" portion of the process may often depend on understanding some of the behavioral theories which we will not treat in this introduction to leadership. References and bibliography will be provided so that readers who wish to do so may participate in further study. The third part of the process calls for what transformational leaders do. They act, and the frequency of their action depends on the frequency of their observation and accounting for events in their units. The presentation of the cases is intended to provide a clear and direct understanding of how leaders act, both good and bad, and in that process instill a long lasting and formative leadership lesson. In each of the cases to be presented, participants will be faced with a real life leadership challenge. You will have the opportunity to decide what is happening, to account for what is happening, and finally, to discuss and decide on a course of action. While we will limit the discussion of the behavioral theories, we still should consider the simplest of these theories, the Ethic of Reciprocity. Many of the behavioral issues underlying leadership problems can be addressed by this approach, which is nothing more than what we learned in childhood as "The Golden Rule".

THE LEADERS THOUGHT AND ACTION PROCESS

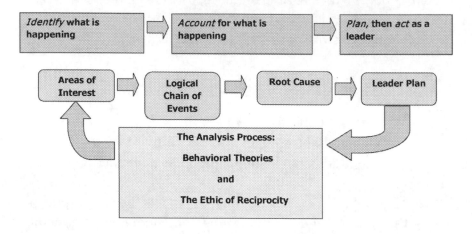

In identifying areas of interest, we need only understand that they are issues which compel a leader to act. They may be positive or negative, but often present themselves as some sort of a problem and thus demand action. As leaders, we must apply the proper action. Acting too quickly is often a problem, and acting too aggressively or too slowly can also cause difficulty for the leader.

The analysis process is simply a leader taking *humanity* into account by any one of many means available, whether detailed and intense study of the theories of behavior or the inherent humanity implied in the Ethic of Reciprocity. (The Golden Rule) In the analysis process, the leader must understand the behavioral concepts which affect his group. He must then apply a concept to address his area of interest.

Root cause knowledge comes to us as a reactive event, telling us something has gone wrong in our process. It often appears as a distinct problem in safety, morale, inefficiency, or one of many other reasons. Root cause is therefore an indicator of past events, but it is also a predictor of future events. In the chemical process industry, as well as in military operational planning, it is very helpful, sometimes critical when planning operations to ask the question "What if . . . ?" and insert the failure of a project event or a delayed timeline. In the continuous process of chemical operations, this is typically done by a HAZOPS[20] review in which a new plant design is submitted to a panel of engineers who ask those "what if" questions. Aboard ship, the Navy uses hypothetical failures of equipment to train operators. This is straightforward if not simple when dealing with mechanical and electrical objects. It is far less straightforward and simple when dealing with human beings.

- ○ **Try to recall a challenging event or problem occurring either now or recently within your organization and apply this process to it. Share and discuss the outcome with other participants. Was the outcome positive or negative?**
- ○ **Review the open system theory of the group and relate it to this process. In particular, view the open system approach as an overlay to the Leader Thought Process.**
- ○ **Construct a model of your own organization which corresponds to the components of the model of the open system theory for your group. Identify the various components and define their positive and negative aspects upon the leadership process as you perceive it in your organization.**
- ○ **Review case #27, (OODA LOOPS) and integrate it into the open system characterization of your group and the Leader Thought Process.**

(*This is a major piece of work and should be closely mentored and attempted as a team. Special care should be taken to ensure a complete description of each of the elements in the model and to have the participants develop these.*)

THE NEW LEADER AUDIT

CASE OBJECTIVES

- ○ To provide the new leader with a structured framework to assess their new responsibilities
- ○ When a new leader assumes responsibility of a group, what are the considerations necessary to begin a leadership plan? How soon can you begin assessing the situation and how quickly may you begin working as a true leader as opposed to a transactional place holder?
- ○ The processes of assuming new responsibilities for a group are very important and they call for skill in observation and assessment in several areas.

Culture—What is the culture? Is it careful, risk oriented, supportive, critical, or judgmental?

Morale—Does the group seem purposeful, fulfilled, eager?

Metrics—Is there a reasonable and fair standard for gauging productivity and success?

Trust and Verify—Your first experience with a new group calls for trust on some issues, and verification on others. That simply means that you may decide to trust people for non-critical items, at least until and unless they prove untrustworthy. This allows you to gauge the various group members and assess their capabilities. Critical issues may call for your close scrutiny and verification. It's up to you to decide which categories apply to the various tasks.

Standards and Procedures—Are there appropriate and usable standards and procedures in place? Are they being followed? If not, they must be developed.

Development Track—Does your organization support the individual's personal development? Is there a path on which individuals can set out to achieve greater responsibility?

Safety—Does the organization respect the safety of individuals? Does it practice safe work habits and reward safety performance?

Ethics—Does the organization and group follow ethical values? Have you been asked to do something which you find unethical?

Motivation Activity: What Do People Want From Their Jobs?

Objective

- To identify what motivates people to work.

Give each learner a copy of the table below. Divide the learners into small groups of three or four. Ask each learner to rank each item under the column titled "Individual" from 1 to 10, with 1 being the most important and 10 being the least important. [21]

Individual Factors	Group Factors	What do people want from their jobs?
_____	_____	Promotion in the Company
_____	_____	Tactful Discipline
_____	_____	Job Security
_____	_____	Help with Personal Problems
_____	_____	Personal Loyalty of Supervisor
_____	_____	High Wages
_____	_____	Full Appreciation of Work Done
_____	_____	Good Working Conditions
_____	_____	Feeling of Being In on Things
_____	_____	Interesting Work

When they have completed the ranking, have each group total the average individual weights within their group. Rank the 10 items under the column titled "Group."

Inform the group that this same scale has been given to thousands of workers across the country. Their ranking is as follows:

Supervisors ranked the items in this order:

1. High Wages
2. Job Security
3. Promotion in the Company
4. Good Working Conditions
5. Interesting Work
6. Personal Loyalty of Supervisor
7. Tactful Discipline
8. Full Appreciation of Work Being Done
9. Help on Personal Problems
10. Feeling of Being In On Things

However, when employees were given the same exercise, their rankings tended to follow this pattern:

1. Full Appreciation of Work Being Done
2. Feeling of Being In On Things
3. Help on Personal Problems
4. Job Security
5. High Wages
6. Interesting Work
7. Promotion in the Company
8. Personal Loyalty of Supervisor
9. Good Working Conditions
10. Tactful Discipline

Discussion Questions

1. **In comparing the different ratings, what might account for the different opinion?**
2. **What might be the cause of the supervisor's rankings being so different from the employees?**
3. **If this survey was given to your department, what would the results be?**

This survey is based on works by Susan Herrington, North Tennessee Private Industry Council in Clarksville, Tenn.

ASLEEP ON WATCH

> "Effective leadership is putting first things first. Effective management is discipline, carrying it out."
>
> **Stephen Covey**[22]

CASE OBJECTIVES

- ○ To discuss the ease with which new leaders sometimes use power
- ○ To recognize the use of power as an only resort is sometimes wrong, and to inform new leaders in the use of creative sanctions

CONTEXT

In 1968 the USS Constellation, an aircraft carrier was operating in the San Diego area and preparing for an extended deployment to the combat zone in Vietnam. The ship was completing a very arduous ten-day workup prior to leaving the states, and the work schedule was aggressive. The crew had been working 12 to 14 hour days, and the men were exhausted. The ship was entering port in the crowded channel around Point Loma and the Naval Air Station. After docking, the Engineering Officer of the Watch came up to the bridge to tell an officer that two of his men, who had been standing watch in the emergency steering stations aft, were found sleeping at their stations. He found that hard to believe, as the two sailors had shown fine discipline at all times and never been problems. They came up to the bridge and admitted that they had in fact fallen asleep at their stations. The emergency steering station is a backup for the main steering. The port (left) and right (starboard) stations were two small closet-sized compartments with a rudder indicator on the forward bulkhead (wall). The only job of the watch stander was to be available in the event that the main steering failed. Then, through a sound-powered phone, the bridge would give rudder commands to the emergency steering watch standers. There were no radios or magazines allowed, and only a metal folding chair for comfort. The stations were just above the propellers and anyone sitting in the stations would hear the constant steady hum as the huge bronze screws beat the water. It was a recipe for sleep.

Sleeping on watch is a serious offense. In this case, had the men not been alert enough to respond, and a steering casualty had occurred in the narrow channel entering port, there could have been serious consequences. The two men were referred to Captain's Mast, also known as Non-Judicial Punishment, a hearing conducted by the Commanding Officer of the ship. In this proceeding, the sailors can be given time in the ship's brig, extra duty, reduction in grade, loss of ½ of base pay for one month, and confinement on bread and water for three days.

- **Do you have any suggestions for improving the conditions of the emergency steering spaces and the rules governing the watch area?**
- **If you were the sailor's division officer, how would you apply punishment? Why?**

Several days later, the charges were brought against the two offenders. It was late at night and the Captain was sitting in his chair on the bridge and reviewing the charges for the next mast. He called the division officer over and asked him what his thoughts were about punishment for the two sailors.

- **What is the purpose of the Captain asking the division officer for his thoughts?**

The Captain knows that the division officer is new to the role. He intends to use the event to improve the leadership skills of the Lieutenant, and to provide the proper application of discipline to the two sailors.

- You are the division officer. Recommend a plan of discipline.
- Consider asking the offenders to recommend a written plan of how they might avoid falling asleep in such a monotonous and isolated situation.

The division officer replied that sleeping on watch was a very serious offense and that he thought they should "throw the book at them". The Captain looked up from the paperwork with a steady eye and told him that he thought more of him. "Sir? ", "Lieutenant" he said, "The book is what you use when you don't know what else to do." He went on to inform him that he had seen the two on bridge duty and thought they looked like a couple of good sailors. He said that he had some concern about giving them a maximum punishment because he did not like the idea of having them think they had one chance in the Navy and they had blown it. He went on to say that he thought they knew very well that they had messed up, and would probably never do it again. He also reminded the Lieutenant that most of the ship had been putting in extremely long hours. But, he told him, it was his call, and he would back him completely no matter what he decided. He became conflicted trying to decide what to do, and then realized that the Captain was trying to teach him something. He decided on a minimum punishment, which would be several days of extra duty and a suspended reduction in rank as long as they completed the next six months with no infractions.

The two sailors appeared at Captains Mast, shaking visibly in the presence of the Commanding Officer, who had the power to confine them to the ships brig for three days on bread and water, or a number of other penalties. He took the papers in hand and read the charges. "Sleeping on watch; it's a damned serious offense in the United States Navy. If it were my decision, I would throw the book at you. But your Lieutenant believes that you two are worth saving, and I have to go with his recommendation, as he knows you better than I do. Do not appear here again"! As they left the proceedings, the two sailors were showering the Lieutenant with a chorus of "thank you" as they walked down the passageway. "We will never let that happen again, sir." The Lieutenant smiled inside. The Captain had made him the hero, cast himself as the bad guy, earned his respect for his leadership ability, and taught a very important lesson. It was pure genius on his part.

- **What are the potential consequences if the division officer does "throw the book" at the two sailors?**
- **Discuss the differences and outcomes between the "throw the book" plan and the actual resolution of the issue at Captain's Mast.**

The lessons of this event are numerous. One is that because there was a strict transactional culture with clear regulations and expectations, there was also some leeway to work on a transformational event. The fear of the "book" made it all possible. Because of that event, the Lieutenant had some "leadership capital". The Captain taught him something that he still remembered after many years. In a pure transactional culture, the rule would have won out. There would have been no discussion between the Captain and the Lieutenant. The two offenders would have gone to mast, the book would have been brought out, and the sentence duly read and carried out. Leadership capital is what happens when you have a one-on-one discussion with the involved party. You inform them what could happen, and then the two of you open up honestly with each other. You share the two sides of the story, you hear each other's viewpoint, and generally, you learn something you didn't know. Both of you emerge from that with strengthened trust. If you reach a settlement less severe than "the book", everyone wins. Another lesson is that just because there is a maximum penalty, it doesn't mean that it has to be used. The restraint of a leader often shows confidence in the individual being disciplined, and now, the individual has a certain relationship with the leader that might not have existed before.

While this example is one with a good result and a bending of the rules, there are certain situations that will not allow a leader such flexibility. Blatant disregard of certain procedures cannot be tolerated. Drug use is one of those, and violation of certain safety regulations is another. It's the leader's job to assess the meaning and intent of their standards, and apply the proper leadership in each event.

THE GUNNY'S FIRST SALUTES

"Sentiment rules the world, and he who fails to take that into account can never hope to lead."

Napoleon Bonaparte

CASE OBJECTIVES

○ To recognize that emotion, no matter what the system structure calls for, remains a basic human quality which must be taken into account

CONTEXT

It is customary in the Naval Aviation Officer Candidate School at Pensacola for the Marine Gunnery Sergeant who trained the young candidates to grant them their first salutes immediately after the commissioning ceremony. It is an interesting change of status, one full of symbolism and tradition. The grizzled gunny, who shouted and prodded and drove them for sixteen weeks, is now a subordinate in rank. Each of them stepped off of the platform with a silver dollar in their pocket and paused briefly before the gunny, taking their first salutes as officers from him in exchange for the silver dollar. As they gathered after the ceremony, one of the newly commissioned officers asked another if he got a good look at the "gunny". He replied that he had not, and asked why. He was certain that the gunny had tears in his eyes. The new officer marveled at that revelation. How could it be that this tough old man, wounded twice at the Inchon landings in Korea, who had trained hundreds of Marines and fought with valor, had such a sentimental touch?

○ **How can you account for the display of sentiment by the rugged combat veteran?**
○ **What lessons does this event provide for evaluating the process of joining the typical organization?**

At the time of the graduation, the Vietnam War was beginning to increase in intensity. Of the thirty members of the Officer Class, one would die in training and two more in combat. The old Marine had seen it all before, and knew what the group faced in the coming months. He had a feeling of pride in his efforts to shape the new officers, but also held a feeling of sadness for what he knew was coming.

- **What part does emotion play in leadership?**
- **Is it an appropriate attribute?**
- **Under what conditions may emotion become an inappropriate quality?**

GENERAL LEE TO THE REAR

"Regard your soldiers as your children, and they will follow you into the deepest valleys; look on them as your own beloved sons, and they will stand by you even unto death."

Sun Tzu

CASE OBJECTIVES

- To provide the participant with a basic recognition of the qualities of leaders and followers

CONTEXT

During the American Civil War, General Robert E. Lee provided leadership of the Confederate Armies. A graduate of West Point and veteran of the Mexican Campaign, Lee was revered by the troops under his command. West of Fredericksburg Virginia was a forested area known as The Wilderness. As Lee faced the numerical superiority of General Ulysses Grant, he made a decision as to the manner of deploying his troops. The advantage Grant had was numbers, and in open ground he would have efficiency of maneuver. Lee therefore decided to engage in the heavily wooded areas of the Wilderness.

Early on the morning after the first engagement, the Union forces launched into the Confederate lines, eager to finish off the rebel forces. Confederate soldiers had begun to flee the battle in terror. Lee understood at once the gravity of his situation. Riding to the front, he questioned the soldiers. "Who are you, my boys?", "Texas boys" they shouted. Lee greeted them with "Hurrah for Texas", and began to lead them back to their lines at the front.[23] The soldiers quickly realized that Lee himself was now in danger, and began to urge him to return to the rear. Unyielding, the General continued until one of his aides took the reins of Lee's horse and compelled his return to safety.

- ○ **Should Lee have risked himself in this way?**
- ○ **What traits do Lee's soldiers exhibit? Are they followers or subordinates?**

Lee, by his humble manners, had endeared himself to the men he commanded. They were followers. To them, he was regarded as a leader, not only a General who commanded subordinates.

LEE'S DESCRIPTION OF A LEADER

"The forbearing use of power does not only form the touchstone, but the manner in which an individual enjoys certain advantages over others is the test of a true gentleman.

The power which the strong have over the weak, the magistrate over the citizen, the employer over the employed, the educated over the unlettered, the experienced over the confiding, even the clever over the silly-the forbearing or inoffensive use of all this power or authority, or the total absence of it when the case admits it, will show the gentleman in plain light. The gentleman does not needlessly or unnecessarily remind an offender of a wrong he may have committed against him. He can not only forgive, he can forget; and he strives for that nobleness of self and mildness of character which impart sufficient strength to let the past be the past.

A true gentleman of honor feels humbled himself when he cannot help humbling others."

BODY COUNTS IN VIETNAM

"The most fundamental incompetence in the Vietnam War was the misapplication of the social and mental model of an industrial process to human warfare"[24]

Jonathan Shay MD PhD

CASE OBJECTIVES

- To illustrate the length to which the transactional can be carried and the limits of its effectiveness

CONTEXT

For most of the American involvement in the Vietnam War, Robert McNamara served as the Secretary of Defense. McNamara was a Harvard educated policy analyst, and he instituted management oriented statistical standards for the military. With the adoption of these standards, the use of the body count became a primary indicator for military officers in gauging the effectiveness of combat operations. Vietnam was different in the sense that the acquiring of territory in North Vietnam was never an objective. The contested territory was South Vietnam, and the enemy was already present. This was the logic behind the body count, and it soon became a primary success indicator.

- **What problems do the use of a numerical indicator such as body counts in a combat situation present?**
- **Is the body count metric able to account for factors other than those most easily observed?**
- **Is it a reliable metric for something as complex as a war?**
- **Are quotas always good in a business setting? Does the quantitative approach always serve the best interests of the organization?**

- ○ **Discuss the variances between the goals of the Generals directing the fight at a high level and the troopers conducting the fight directly, and how the body count can produce problems in this regard.**

The use of the body count proved to be a false transactional metric in Vietnam, as it would in wars which are usually waged for complex political and social reasons. It was also detrimental to morale as bodies were often kept until they were able to be counted and reviewed by higher ranks, and some were even dug up for presentation. In at least one division, quotas were assigned for body counts. For example, a certain mission required a certain number of enemy dead. This changed the underlying rationale for the mission. Instead of serving as a blocking force, a reconnaissance, or an intelligence gathering mission, the quota overrode the mission purpose. Most of all though, it failed to account for the complex web of political, social, and economic factors, all of which needed to be considered in whether or not the war was proceeding in the favor of the US and South Vietnam. To truly understand the utility of a measurement, we have to drill down deep enough into an organizations structure and long term vision and purpose. In Vietnam, the body count was marginally useful as an indicator of local tactics, but did not reveal the complex issues in effect.

NORMANDY 1944[25]

"The power of example is very important to people under stress."

British General Sir John Hackett

CASE OBJECTIVES

- To understand the nature of responsibility and its qualities
- To acquaint the participant with the power of leading by example
- To develop the art of the leader to show and not to simply tell

CONTEXT

In the late summer of 1944, a young Infantry Captain found himself in command of a company of US soldiers advancing against the Germans in the breakout from Normandy. He had already distinguished himself as a leader. He had been with the company for two years, through training in the California desert and the Normandy beaches. He knew his men and felt a deep obligation to bring them home safely.

The unit had advanced steadily and they were now in position attempting to move forward. They had attempted to move without success and had taken casualties. The various companies of the battalion were dispersed and communicating with field telephones. The Captain's phone buzzed and he received orders from the new Battalion Operations Officer, a Major, to move out with a squad of men and establish an observation post on the hill the Germans controlled. The Captain informed the Operations Officer that any attempt to move forward would be foolish. The Operations Officer replied that this was a direct order, and the Captain replied that he was refusing it. A short time later, the Captain's phone buzzed again. A platoon leader in the company had been contacted by the Operations Officer and ordered to move out. The platoon leader understood the risk and wanted guidance from the Captain. "Stay put, everybody stay put" the Captain commanded.

- ○ **Place yourself in the position of the Captain. What will you do? Must you follow the order?**
- ○ **Does the new Ops Officer know the facts of the situation? More importantly, does he understand the facts?**
- ○ **What are the Captain's obligations to the Battalion? To his own men? Do they conflict?**
- ○ **What are his choices?**
- ○ **What do you think he will do?**

The Captain told his Sergeant what he intended to do and the two set out for the Battalion Command Post. There, the Captain informed the Ops Officer that he was ready to carry out the orders to place a squad on the hill. Pointing to the Ops Officer, he said "My Sergeant and I will go, and you will come with us." The Ops Officer could hardly refuse an order he just gave, and joined the two. The Captain drove and the Sergeant manned the mounted .30 caliber machine gun. In seconds after they left the cover of their positions, the German post above them began to rain artillery down as they tried to hit the jeep and the three American soldiers. It was apparent to the Operations Officer that the three men were soon in a dangerous, perhaps fatal, situation. The Captain drove on; ignoring the fury around them, and the Operations Officer soon asked him to turn around. "Is that an order?" the Captain replied. "Yes, yes", responded the Operations Officer. "Turn around now, damn it!" The Captain turned the jeep around and the three drove back to Battalion Headquarters. The Captain addressed the Operations Officer angrily. "These are my men. I am responsible for their conduct. Never give an order to me or my men that you are not willing to carry out yourself!"

ACTIVITY QUESTIONS

- ○ **Discuss the emotional response of the Captain's soldiers once they learn of this event.**
- ○ **Discuss the reasons for the actions of the Captain. What part did his close attachment to his men and their training over a two-year period have on his methods?**
- ○ **Discuss the effective use of conflict in this situation.**
- ○ **Was this overall event necessary? Could any other method have been applied by the Captain? By the Battalion Operations Officer?**
- ○ **Compare and contrast this event as it was handled in the military and how a typical stressful event might be handled in the average corporation.**

Imagine the response of the men under the command of that Captain. What was the effect on their morale? Although this Captain had established himself as a leader of character much earlier, this particular incident could only have enhanced his standing. He showed two different types of courage, moral and physical. He also displayed a quick genius. There is little to be gained from a debate under such critical conditions. He chose to prove his point with his presence, and to teach the Operations Officer in the only manner possible. Years later, when a member of the company met the Captain's son, he told him that as long as the Captain led them, they felt they would return home safely. He also told them that during training, they men hated him because he drove them so hard, but that when they entered combat, they suddenly understood. You need to be present to lead. You must understand the conditions under which your people labor. Leaders at a distance have little to offer. There were Generals on the Normandy beaches in the most difficult moments of the invasion. While it is true that at some level the leader has to separate himself from the action, it is always a positive factor to be among the people doing the work. Distance becomes a negative factor when the leader assumes that he knows what is going on, or when he fails to understand the true nature of the work without any exposure to it. Simply put, you learn things when you spend time with your people.

There are numerous lessons to be gained here. The first is the genius of the Captain in his approach toward the situation. This was not a time for debate, but action. The only way he could show the Operations Officer the difficulty of the situation was to place him in position that would show, and not merely tell, of the problem caused by such an order. Had the Captain chosen to debate or argue, he probably would have created a more difficult situation for himself and ultimately for his troops. In this instance, he showed remarkable courage by exposing himself to the same fire, some might argue unnecessarily. But moral courage is often more difficult to act on than is physical. The Captain displayed both. His troops saw the event unfold, and knew of his courage and concern for their welfare. The Battalion Operations Officer learned, in a few short minutes of terror, why his order was foolish. You cannot lead from the rear. Years later, the Sergeant was visiting the Captain's son. He said, "We hated your father in training in the States. When we got into combat we understood his methods. We felt that with him leading us, we had a chance to survive." This young Captain was a leader, and his soldiers knew and trusted him with their lives. Leadership is about many things. It is based on good judgment, action, and a genuine love for those you wish to lead. This Captain displayed all three. A fourth and rarely discussed element is instinct. Instinct is an intuitive action, often relied on when events present themselves in such a pressing manner that there is no time for reflection or discussion. Instinct loomed large in the actions of this officer. He trusted his instincts and acted on them. Another lesson is that the Captain understood just how new the Major was to the tempo of combat. His genius was to deliver an indelible method of instruction that would "teach" the Major in a most effective manner. Through his quick and decisive action, the Captain provided a lesson to the Major. This brief but effective lesson also gave the Major a look at the reality of combat, and provided him with a reason to watch and learn from a subordinate. Sometimes that is all that is necessary to learn how things really work in a new and difficult environment. Often you, as a leader, will have to accept training from a follower who really knows his job. This event also illustrates the very effective use of conflict, which is typically avoided by the transactional paradigm. In this event, conflict was employed to teach and to deliver a very effective and compelling result to the problem confronting the young Captain.

HARDCORE RECONDO SIR!

> "The best leaders . . . almost without exception and at every level are master users of stories and symbols."
>
> **Tom Peters**

CASE OBJECTIVES

- ○ To illustrate the range of performance demonstrated by transformational leadership
- ○ To demonstrate the use of symbols and recognition in a leadership process

CONTEXT

In January of 1969, Lt. Colonel David Hackworth took command of an infantry battalion in Vietnam.[26] The unit had fallen into a terrible state of morale and inefficiency, and Hackworth had been given a challenge to return it to combat excellence. While there were numerous challenges to combat efficiency, Hackworth also had the experience to understand the need for improved morale. Among his first orders were to return to the military custom of the salute. As each soldier saluted, he greeted the senior with "Hardcore Recondo Sir", to which the officer replied with a profane "No f . . . ing slack". He had one of his lieutenants design and order small metal pins with the battalion insignia. These would be worn on uniforms, and the same design was painted on helmets and the battalion vehicles, company and battalion areas. He created battalion stationery, and ordered soldiers to shave each day in the rest areas.

There were early objections and complaints, but eventually the changes began to be adopted. While all this was occurring, Hackworth began to retrain the troops on basic soldiering. He wanted their reactions at the squad level to be automatic when confronted with action. Among the tenets he issued to his officers and NCO's were the following:

- o   Fight smart, never be in a hurry
- o   Lead from up front
- o   Set the example
- o   Take care of your troops before yourself
- o   Keep up the good communications

In his personal leadership, Hackworth exemplified the instructions he issued. Hackworth operated on the concept that there were no bad soldiers, only bad officers. Two instances serve as examples of his dedication to the welfare of his soldiers. Hackworth had been speaking with a trooper who told him that his feet were terribly painful. When he asked why, the soldier informed Hack that he had unusually small feet, and that he had never worn boots that fit. The supply officer of the battalion was met with a storm created by Hackworth. He was told that if he had to contact every outfit in Vietnam, he had better find a pair of boots for the soldier. He did, locating a pair of boots used by Army nurses in the correct size. The boot issue was of concern for infantry, and soon Hackworth's lead was being followed by his junior officers and NCO's. His battalion Executive Officer noticed a soldier wearing a pair of boots with the toes worn out and his feet exposed. He asked him what size boots he wore, and as it happened, they were the same size as the XO. The XO removed his boots and gave them to the trooper.

- o   **Discuss the use of symbols as effective morale builders. How do they support the greater mission?**
- o   **How fast does communication spread when a leader performs a transactional event that is perceived to be negative?**
- o   **What about transformational events? Do they spread as rapidly as negatively perceived transactional events?**

SKUNKS AND SYCOPHANTS
(TO BE PRESENTED WITH "RESPECT THESE")

> "I can bear to hear of imputed or real errors. The man who wishes to stand well in the opinion of others must do this, because he is thereby enabled to correct his faults or remove the prejudices which are imbibed against him."[27]
>
> **George Washington**

CASE OBJECTIVES

- To acquaint new leaders with the necessity for humility and open and honest communication with the group

CONTEXT

Lt. General Hal Moore was the subject of the movie "We Were Soldiers Once, and Young". Moore discusses a concept he called "Bringing a skunk to your picnic" in the book of the same name. Each time Moore took command of a new unit, he searched for the one person who would tell him what he thought, regardless of whether or not it was a comment favorable to Moore. He called this person his "skunk at the picnic". To be selected as his skunk, the person would have to be courageous and honest. The purpose of the appointment of the skunk was to invite criticism and the use of collective intelligence. Criticism is very important to a leader. If followers are going to be affected by the actions and policies of the leader, they may see things in his decisions that he cannot. In large organizations, this may be very important, even critical in revealing possible problems. It is also important to let the organization know that there is an informal channel to the boss which is useful in making their concerns known. But perhaps the most important effect of the skunk is that the leader is not placing himself above the followers. He establishes himself as someone whose ego is in order, and unafraid of criticism. Moore said that he did not always follow the recommendations of his skunks, but he always listened to them. Inviting criticism and using the collective intelligence of the group are the fundamentals behind this process.

- ○ **Does this description of the "skunk" fit the traditional view of the manner in which decisions are made in the military?**
- ○ **Compare the actions of leaders you have worked for. Would they be more comfortable with a skunk or a sycophant?**
- ○ **Which do you prefer? Which do you need?**

You should understand that as a leader, you can only succeed if you utilize the entire power of your group of followers. If you cut them off from communication, you have lost the collective intelligence of the group. The answers to most of the problems you face are typically to be found somewhere within the group. You can facilitate the process by communication and encouragement among the team. If you are the 10th person and leader of a 9-person team, and isolate yourself from communication with them, you have denied yourself access to 90% of the collective intelligence of the team.

The history of the skunk in the military goes far back in U.S. tradition. In his biography of George Washington, author Ron Chernow quotes Washington on the subject.

JOHN MCCAIN IN HANOI

> Goodness is about character—integrity, honesty, kindness, generosity, moral courage, and the like. More than anything else, it is about how we treat other people.
>
> **Dennis Prager**

CASE OBJECTIVES

- To provide an example of how personal honor and virtue supports leadership in a situation of great stress

CONTEXT

John McCain is best known as a US Senator and Presidential Candidate. Before his service in the Senate, McCain spent twenty years in the Navy as an attack pilot. In this role he was shot down over Vietnam and captured in 1967 and returned home in 1973. During his tenure as a POW, McCain, who had already been grievously injured and barely survived, underwent brutal torture by his captors. To this day, his arms are so severely damaged that he cannot raise them above his head.

At some point in his captivity, his captors learned that he was the son and grandson of Admirals. During his captivity, his father was promoted to Commander-in-Chief Pacific. In that role, he commanded all US forces in the area, including air, land, and sea. It was then that his captors came to McCain and offered him an early release, hoping to gain some bargaining power with the US during the peace negotiations. The senior Naval Officer among the POW's was then Captain James Stockdale. Stockdale had issued orders among the POW's that the only releases were to be for medical reasons. McCain knew this, but he had a personal reason to refuse the Vietnamese offer. His friend, Navy Lt Cdr Everett Alvarez, was the longest held among the POW's. McCain chose to stay and endure more years of torture because he felt he could not face Alvarez in the future if he accepted an early release.

- o **What are the differences if any between personal honor and honor under orders? McCain had both.**
- o **What effect might McCain's action have had on other POW's, especially Alvarez?**
- o **Discuss your own thoughts regarding this action by McCain. Would you have performed as he did under these circumstances?**

THE SIGNALMAN'S COURT MARTIAL

"It is impossible to imagine anything which better becomes a ruler than mercy."

Seneca

CASE OBJECTIVES

- ◦ To illustrate the need for thorough and rigorous examination prior to judgment
- ◦ To provide an examination of the role of a leader in a situation involving organizational conflict

CONTEXT

You are a Lieutenant Commander in the Navy. As a collateral duty, you have been assigned to act as Senior Officer in a Special Court Martial. The accused is a Signalman 3rd Class. During a port visit in the Philippines, The Signalman failed to return to the ship, returning only 45 days later when the ship returned to port once more. He is charged with Unauthorized Absence. The Uniform Code of Military Justice is very clear in cases such as this. If you were not there, and have not suffered injury to prevent you from being present, you are charged with Unauthorized Absence. There are few mitigating circumstances if any. The maximum sentence that a Special Court Martial can impose are six months confinement at hard labor, six months loss of pay, reduction to the lowest possible rank, and dismissal from the service with a dishonorable discharge. The colloquial term for this maximum punishment is "six-six-and kick". Most cases of UA result in at least a portion of the above consequences, if not all. The members of the Court were not expecting much from the young Signalman. The case seemed pretty simple as they convened the Court. The Trial Counsel, or prosecutor, presented the simple facts. The sailor was absent from his duties and the ship for 45 days. It seemed straightforward. The

Defense Counsel then presented a surprise to the Court. He put the sailor on the witness stand. For nearly two hours, the sailor told his story, and the Court listened with rapt attention. He had married on the day he graduated from High School and his Navy Enlistment began about one week later. The couple traveled to San Diego, where he attended Boot Camp and she worked as a waitress. They had about six weeks together in a tiny apartment before his orders came for sea duty. For a time things seemed to be going well. She wrote to him, and he responded with letters of his own. When in a rare port visit, he made sure he tried to call her each time. Then the letters slowed, and finally stopped. One night in the Philippines, he waited in line for two hours to call home. When he finally got through, a man answered the phone. At this point in the testimony, the sailor, who looked like a recruiting poster, began to shake, and finally wept. The entire Court looked away in embarrassment at the sight while the sailor continued his story. After the phone call, he went into a bar and drowned his sorrows. He missed the departure of the ship the next day. A young woman who worked at the bar brought him home to her family. Her father was a retired US Navy Chief, and she wanted her father to hear his story and offer advice. He remained with the family for several weeks, just getting away from the Navy, which he felt was responsible for his problems.

Military Courts have two phases, the first part being finding, and the second sentencing. In the first phase, the Court had found him guilty. When the second phase commences the accused has the opportunity to present "mitigating and extenuating circumstances". It's usually hard to find such circumstances in UA cases. Now, the Court had heard the testimony that had caused the young sailor to go over the edge. As the Senior Officer of the Court, you have the power to influence your juniors. You also have a responsibility to uphold the "good order and discipline" of the Navy. Assess your responsibilities and decide what you will recommend to your colleagues. Remember that you cannot order the result as the President, as each member of the court votes by secret written ballot. The court convened for sentencing after having found the defendant guilty of the Unauthorized Absence of 47 days.

- ○ **You have a wide range of options. You may go for the maximum "six-six and kick" or anything less, including no punishment.**
- ○ **What option will best serve the Navy in this case?**
- ○ **Do you have an obligation to the young sailor? Discuss and defend your decision.**

The court sentenced the defendant to 47 days of emergency leave. They told him that his record until now was excellent, but that he had found himself in a situation which was overwhelming. He was ordered to go back to the base in the US and report to the Legal Officer and Chaplain for guidance as necessary during each day of his emergency leave.

While we cannot allow all overwhelming personal issues to take precedence in a work environment, we must nevertheless be aware of external circumstances that affect the ability to work. The military has great experience in the handling of young people in those circumstances, and when and where it is possible and practical, the military applies appropriate leadership to the moment and to the circumstance. Leaders bear at least some of the responsibility for the success or failure of their followers.

LEMAY'S GRIPE SESSIONS

"It is curious that physical courage should be so common in the world and moral courage so rare."

Mark Twain

CASE OBJECTIVES

○ To provide leaders with an example that leadership under stress may necessitate the need for frank and passionate communication
○ To show the potential for a teaching and learning moment in a group setting

CONTEXT

Most public knowledge of General Curtis Lemay is based on the popular media portrayal of him as a cigar chomping, bombastic, blood and guts leader. But as with many things, that popular image is not altogether accurate. Lemay was a remarkable leader who committed to learning from every mistake, every mission, and every airman in his command. Learning was critical. To that end, he broke military tradition by instituting the "closed-door briefing" at the conclusion of every mission. In these sessions, no holds were barred. Airmen dissected not only their performance, but that of their leader. No one would be reprimanded for his comments and criticisms of Lemay.

○ **What are the advantages of such a process?**
○ **Can you think of a post-event use of such a process in your own organization?**
○ **As a leader, what are the disadvantages or challenges in such a situation and how might you handle them?**

Learning can be stifled by excessive structure. By breaking with tradition, Lemay encouraged open and honest communication. It is rare that two people will view an event in exactly the same perspective. By this break with tradition, Lemay was able to learn how everyone in the group perceived the problem and its solutions. Lemay also knew that he had to make every attempt to shorten the war by precision bombing. This meant that he had to employ the bomber pilot's version of the fighter pilot's "OODA Loop" (Observe-Orient-Decide-Act). By concentrating these learning sessions, he gained useful knowledge. His primary goal was to be always ahead of the enemy in his learning. This goal was superior to tradition and the usual military courtesy. It was about prevailing against the enemy. Nothing else was as important.

Learning may have been the primary goal of these sessions, but it was not the only element of value. By gathering the crews together after the tense atmosphere of a combat mission, Lemay offered a time to vent the tension somewhat. One of the practices of the USAAF post mission was to offer crews a shot of whiskey. Lemay offered more of a team building approach by offering his crews the chance to use him as a psychological target. The gripe sessions were team building events too. By taking all of the crews together, Lemay distributed the lessons learned on the mission all at once, and each of the crews came to understand that they were not alone in their feelings and observations.

WASHINGTON AT THE SECOND BATTLE OF TRENTON

"We convince by our presence."

Walt Whitman

CASE OBJECTIVES

- To demonstrate the need for presence as a factor of morale
- To demonstrate the need for absolute truth in determining the outcome of an important evolution

CONTEXT

In January of 1777, the Continental Army under Washington held Trenton after a decisive victory. The British and their Hessian mercenaries massed against a blocking force of 1,000 Continentals holding the Post Road into Trenton. There were another 6,000 Continentals on the heights above Trenton, holding the high ground with artillery. The blocking force was to delay the British advance as long as possible and then fall back across a narrow bridge across a creek. The mass of the blocking force began their maneuver at dusk and the little bridge was packed with soldiers. Washington knew the risk. If the blocking force panicked, the possibility for casualties would mount. They had to continue their fire against the British momentum while crossing the bridge into safety, and then join with the larger force on the heights. Washington believed it important enough that he decided to be there to oversee the maneuver and with his presence, assure the troops under his command. He stationed himself on his horse, at the head of the bridge. Unmoving and calm, he gave confidence to his soldiers and remained until the maneuver was completed.

As we study the actions of leaders, we will begin to see certain qualities reveal themselves. Presence and courage will most likely be among our top choices. Leadership involves having the judgment to understand when those two qualities are required.

- ○ **What, if any, are the substitutes for presence?**
- ○ **Can you use email and photos in the place of presence?**
- ○ **Discuss the attributes of face-to-face communication**

THE COOPER RIVER

"It is by presence of mind in untried emergencies that the native metal of man is tested."

James Russell Lowell

CASE OBJECTIVES

- To provide examples of training and expectations developed by training
- To show how confidence displayed by leaders has a resonance among followers
- To demonstrate that leaders must always be ready to teach and evaluate calmly

CONTEXT

The Commanding Officer of a US Submarine was preparing for a trip up the Cooper River to the Naval Weapons Station prior to a deployment from the Naval Base in Charleston, South Carolina. There the crew would load torpedoes, and return to their berth later in the day. The trip involved a long and winding route up the river, which was a somewhat narrow and congested waterway. Only a week before, another submarine had run aground and damaged its sonar dome in the river. Any accident or significant incident may cost the Captain his command. The underway duty officer for the day in question was a new and untested officer who had just completed the Submarine School Course in New London, Connecticut. No one had seen him perform, and the only information the Commanding Officer had was the young officer's records from Submarine School. A few hours prior to getting underway, the Executive Officer (XO) approached the Commanding Officer and told him that he would replace the young officer with someone more experienced. A collision at sea or a grounding of a ship of the US Navy almost always results in the dismissal of the Commanding Officer and the end of his career.

- ○ **What is the objective of the Executive Officer in this instance?**
- ○ **Do you agree with the Executive Officer? Discuss and defend**.
- ○ **You are the Commanding Officer. What will you do in this instance? Discuss and defend**.

The Commanding Officer told the Executive Officer that he was going to get underway with the duty roster as it was written, with no substitutions.

- ○ **Why do you think the Captain rejected the Executive Officer's recommendation?**

He replied that there was no situation that the young officer could get into that he, the Captain, could not get out of. He also told the XO that he had to begin the assessment of the new officer at some time, and now was a good time to start.

- ○ **What roles do confidence and training play in this case?**
- ○ **How does structure in training provide confidence to a leader?**
- ○ **To a follower?**

The attribute of confidence goes a long way toward producing a competent team environment. Leaders must show confidence in their followers, but they must also display confidence of their own. This Captain stationed himself behind the lookouts on the sail, lit a cigar, and told the new Ensign that he would take the boat upriver. After the loading was done and the ship returned to its berth again, he sat down with the young officer and calmly discussed the evolution, pointing out a few things he would have done differently.

He never interrupted the officer during the evolution, preferring the calm and somewhat relaxed approach after the trip downriver. The Captain also displayed confidence in the Navy system of training. He had been through the Submarine Course years before, and he knew the rigor of the training and had confidence in the structure. This is also an example of how the use of well defined training procedures can instill a certain level of confidence in leaders and followers. The training factor reduces the unknowns to a reasonable level for all the parties, and it also creates a set of reasonable expectations. Properly handled, these expectations are designed to become part of the culture.

WASHINGTON IN THE TRENCHES

> "I used to say of Napoleon that his presence on the field made the difference of forty thousand men."
> **Duke of Wellington**

CASE OBJECTIVES

- ○ To illustrate the power of example and to demonstrate that teaching moments are among the most valuable tools of a leader
- ○ To show that team building requires participation of the leader in certain situations
- ○ To place the trappings of rank and power in the proper perspective

CONTEXT

Warfare during the American Revolution consisted of maneuver and siege. Siege defense had a great deal to do with building breastworks of trenches and fortifications. On one particular day devoted to the construction of trenches, a rider in civilian clothes observed a corporal supervising the trench building, shouting at a group of soldiers as they labored. Curious, he stopped to inquire of the corporal as to why he was not helping. His reply was that he "was a corporal". The civilian apologized for the apparent affront, dismounted, and pitched in to assist. After a time, he finished helping the soldiers and returned to the corporal before going on his way. "Corporal" he said, "the next time you have a task of this type, and not enough men to do it, come to your General, and I will find the soldiers you need".

George Washington later wrote that ". . . the first object of a Captain should be to gain the love of his men by treating them with every possible kindness and humanity, enquiring into their complaints, and when well founded, seeing them redressed. He should often visit those who are sick and speak tenderly to them. The attachment that arises from this kind of attention to the sick and wounded is almost inconceivable."

- ○ **What would the effect of Washington visiting in the trenches and participating in physical work be**? **What do you imagine the troops discussed after this event?**
- ○ **Should a General be doing manual labor among his troops?**
- ○ **What do you think might have been Washington's reason for doing this?**

History is replete with examples of military leaders going in among the troops and participating in the danger, from Lee at Gettysburg, to Alexander the Great, to General Stanley MacChrystal going on patrol in Afghanistan. It tends to be much less prevalent in civilian occupations, and business leaders are often greatly detached from the workplace. Distance does not produce great leaders. There is another reason for Washington's action. Great leaders teach. It is unlikely that the lesson in this case would have been forgotten. If a General will help with the physical labor, so can a corporal.

APPROACHING OKINAWA

"You've got to give loyalty down, if you want loyalty up."
Donald T. Regan

CASE OBJECTIVES

- ○ To demonstrate the full scope and range of responsibility
- ○ To illustrate the quality of downward loyalty and its transformational effects

CONTEXT

A vessel of the US Navy was transiting north from the Philippine Islands to Japan for a rest and recreation period. The transit from the area was almost due north until Okinawa came into radar range, and then the course changed to a northeasterly direction. During the transit, the ship paralleled a time zone that began just about at the westernmost edge of Okinawa. It was a mid-watch, from midnight to four AM, with no vessels in company and few radar contacts. The watch team had a plotted course to follow, and everything seemed in order. They could see the outlying islands of Okinawa on the radar as they approached. At some point the Officer of the Deck (OOD) looked at the radar and expressed concern that the islands seemed too close. He asked the junior officer of the watch to come into the chart house with him. The two of them looked at the chart and the night orders again. The night orders are the courses and speeds ordered by the Captain prior to the evening watches. In those night orders was a "closest point of approach" for the Okinawa area. The ship had clearly begun to exceed the limits of the night orders, but the watch team could not understand why. It was then that they realized that the night orders had been written without taking the time zone change into account. This meant that they should have begun the northeastern leg of their course an hour before they actually started it.

When it becomes necessary to deviate from the night orders, the Captain and Navigator must be notified immediately. It's not usually a pleasant experience, and due to the failure to recognize the time zone problem, this would not be much fun either. The OOD called the Captain, and the Junior Officer of the Deck called the Navigator to tell him what happened. The night orders had been written by the Chief Quartermaster and the first thing the Navigator asked was "Who wrote the orders?" When he was told that the Chief had written them, he said; "Have him come up first thing in the morning. He and I need to have a talk."

- ○ **What is likely to be the outcome of the discussion between the Chief and the Navigator?**
- ○ **Whose responsibility is it to review and approve the Night Orders?**

The Navigator was not pleased with the news. This was an embarrassing mistake which reflected badly on his department. The OOD was informed of the tone of the Navigator's comments, and the OOD responded quickly and decisively. "When the Chief shows up in the morning, you and I will be with him. We had a responsibility to pick up that mistake, but we didn't. The Chief will not face the Navigator alone."

- ○ **What does the OOD's action mean to the Chief?**
- ○ **What leadership trait does the OOD exhibit in this case?**

Loyalty to those whom we hope to lead can be achieved in many ways. As a leader, you can delegate everything but responsibility. You are always responsible. The training, teaching, care and oversight of followers are your responsibilities. In this event, one can readily understand the effect of the OOD joining the Chief and sharing the blame. The word quickly went out that the OOD would not let anyone take the blame for shared mistakes. All of the watch standers who would serve under this OOD would now come to their tasks with a solid understanding that this officer was loyal to them, and would back them up if they did their jobs, even if sometimes mistakes were made. Loyalty is required in both directions. True leaders exemplify this principle and demonstrate it when necessary. There is another element to this case. That is that this OOD took it upon himself to train the JOOD, who was soon to be qualified as an OOD. He wanted him to understand the nature of loyalty to followers too and he made the point clear to the JOOD after the event was over.

BRIGADIER GENERAL KENNETH WALKER

"The basic building block of communications is the feeling that every human being is unique and of value."

Unknown

CASE OBJECTIVES

- ○ A demonstration of how implementation of a new vision requires rigorous on scene analysis accompanied by presence

CONTEXT

Brigadier General Kenneth Walker was an early advocate of the theories of the heavy bomber in war. Walker had joined the Army in 1917. Then only 19 years old, he entered the Air Corps and was commissioned an officer after flight training. Walker was an intense young man, ambitious and driven. He rose slowly in rank in the peacetime years, and in 1934, still a First Lieutenant, he became Commanding Officer of the 9th Bombardment Squadron before promotion to Captain in August 1935. During the ensuing years Walker had a number of staff assignments and attendance at the Army Command and Staff College. It was during these years that Walker and others began to theorize the use of the Army Air Corps as a separate service, and also became advocates of the bombing theory. The attack on Pearl Harbor accelerated the manning levels and promotions of the Army Air Corps, and in 1942 Walker was promoted to Brigadier General and assigned to the South Pacific. The B-17 had only been developed in the years immediately before World War II, and the Army Air Corps had very little experience with the new airplane or the use of heavy bombers in war. Walker doubtless saw the opportunity to test and prove the concept he had formed along with other leaders during peacetime service.

Walker's intensity was evident. From the first hours of his arrival, he committed himself to learning as much as possible about the missions the men under his command were flying, and soon found himself flying with them despite his rank. Walker's superiors were adamant that he not fly the missions with his men, but he continued to share the risks.

- ○ **Why does General Walker fly these missions? Should he?**
- ○ **Evaluate the actions of Walker from the perspective of his Commanding Officer and from that of Walker as his perceived duties as a leader? How and why are they different?**
- ○ **What about the perspective of those who served under Walker?**

He had been rebuked by his commanders for this, but Walker argued that the theory of bombing was new, and he, as an advocate, could not send men on missions unless he understood the challenges involved. Largely because of his participation in missions and other treatment of enlisted men, such as standing in line for meals despite his rank, endeared him to enlisted men and improved communication and suggestions from all ranks.

On 5 January 1943, despite orders to cease flying on combat missions, Walker accompanied the crew of a B-17 on a daylight bombing raid to Rabaul, New Britain. The aircraft was lost. Walker received a posthumous Medal of Honor and remains missing. It would have been his 17th mission.

Kenneth Walker endured the years of slow promotion and growth of the Air Corps while he kept his vision of the role of bombers intact. His assignment to Command was the opportunity he had waited for, and he eagerly embraced the role of study, observation, and participation. Now it was time to see if the theory held up in application. He was a visionary leader, and was unafraid to immerse himself into the missions.

Nowhere in business is there demanded the sacrifice of the military, but too often business leaders fail to fully embrace the applications of their visions, and lose the participation of their followers by remaining remote and distant. Remaining connected is critical, especially when a new strategy or process is being rolled out. Walker did not go on the missions because he lacked trust in the information his followers gave him. Rather, he went because he needed to see the missions from the perspective of a leader. Many military leaders might correctly argue that Walker was lost needlessly. Walker placed great importance on testing the concept he had developed. It was simply the right thing to do. He probably should have ceased flying in combat after a few missions, but his intensity would not allow it. The lesson here is not that we have to die for proof of concept, only that we should be willing to plunge in to where the "rubber meets the road" enough to be certain of its application.

CANDIDATE JONES

> "I learned an awful lot in the Marine Corps—particularly about, I think, how to treat people, lead people—which has played a big role in FedEx. A big part of the employee relations systems and all that we have at our company came from my experience in the service. The Marine Corps is the best when it comes to teaching people how to lead other folks."
>
> **Fred Smith, FED Ex Founder**

CASE OBJECTIVES

- To inform the new leader of the importance of every member of the organization
- To illustrate the importance of group support
- To provide the new leader with the importance of celebrating individual success

CONTEXT

In 1966 I was a newly commissioned Ensign in the Navy. I was in the early phase of flight training in Pensacola, and sitting in an Airframes and Power Plants class taught by a Marine Major. There was a knock at the classroom door, and the Major beckoned for someone to come in. Our former Drill Instructor, a Marine Gunnery Sergeant, entered the room. "Gentlemen" the Major said "the Gunny would like a few words with you." To those who have never experienced training by Marines, you should know that a Marine Gunnery Sergeant/Drill Instructor is probably the closest thing to God on earth. The relationship between a Gunnery Sergeant USMC and his charges is unique. He had been with us all the moments of our day, conducting rifle inspections, teaching us to march, putting us to bed and waking us for the early morning runs. And he was there too, when we finished it all. He stood at the end of the stage and had the privilege to see our success and give us our first salute, and received the customary silver dollar that tradition requires of us. Despite the fact that we were now successfully beyond the Gunny's watchful eyes and strict discipline, we still retained a very healthy reverence for him. The Gunny got right to the point. We had left one of our classmates behind, and the Gunny wanted our participation in an important event.

The Officer Candidate Program at Pensacola was divided into three departments. These were military, academic, and physical fitness. If a candidate fell behind standards in any department, they were held back until they passed, while their class moved on. If they failed to pass, they were ultimately removed from the program. Candidate Jones (not his real name) had been a standout in academics, setting the curve and giving the rest of us a standard of excellence. He had experienced difficulty with the 500 yard obstacle course, though, which many felt was the most difficult element of the physical program. For some weeks he had been held behind, working out every day under the tutelage of the Marine Captain who ran the program. Tomorrow, the Gunny explained, Candidate Jones was to have his last chance at the obstacle course. Our presence was being requested at the course tomorrow afternoon after the last class. We were to be the cheering section.

- ○ **Discuss the motivation of the Gunnery Sergeant. What does his request indicate?**

We understood that this was not really a request. Despite the fact that we now outranked the Gunny, all of us understood the request to be an order. It was an order we understood and received eagerly. Candidate Jones was one of us, and we must retrieve him and bring him back into our band.

The next afternoon at the appointed time, the entire class of new officers assembled at the obstacle course and stood in the sand in our spit shined shoes and highly creased uniforms. We waited for the timer to drop his hand and signal Jones to begin the course. Some of us were to run alongside him and give encouragement, while others would act as timers at each of the key obstacles so that he would know his progress. On what might have been his last day in the Navy, Jones began his career anew. He remained in the Navy and eventually rose to the rank of Captain.

- **Discuss the Gunny's attitude toward the completion of his duty.**
- **What might be the emotions experienced by the newly commissioned officers at the success of Candidate Jones?**
- **Does this event reveal something of the traits of a leader?**

As we will learn in other cases, the military places a great emphasis on personal development. The Gunny did not consider his job as complete without a final attempt to have Candidate Jones succeed. He had been responsible all through the OCS schedule, and now he had one final objective to achieve. He could easily have left Candidate Jones to succeed or fail without his or our participation. The Gunny was invested in the success of Jones, and he utilized his leadership initiative to show support for Jones, and all of us learned something of the importance of teamwork. It is part of the culture of the US Marine Corps that no one is left behind. There will be few who witnessed that event who will not remember that very special moment with fondness.

DOC BRYAN AND THE MAJOR

"One man with courage is a majority."

Thomas Jefferson

CASE OBJECTIVES

- ○ Demonstrates how in intense and chaotic situations, basic values can be overridden or ignored
- ○ To recognize the importance of not only the overall mission, but also the mission and duties of each member of a team
- ○ To illustrate the power of leadership at every level of the group

CONTEXT

In his book, "One Bullet Away-The Making of a Marine Officer" author Nathaniel Fick describes an event that took place during combat in Iraq. His platoon of Reconnaissance Marines had been given orders to take an airfield which was believed to be hostile, and everyone in the area, once they entered, was to be declared hostile. Essentially, the airfield was declared a "free fire zone". In his training at Quantico, Fick had learned that the uses of free fire zones by the military in Vietnam were judged to have been counterproductive and immoral. Yet here he was, preparing to lead his platoon in the very same approach. This was a huge change in the normal rules of engagement, and Fick hesitated, even to the point of considering countermanding the order. He finally relented, hoping that someone at a higher level would have access to information that he did not. The platoon entered the airfield area and prepared to fire at will at anything moving. In the fog of war, someone reported men with rifles opposing the Marines. As the team entered the area, it quickly became evident that there were no men with rifles. The field was deserted, and had been for some time. It was then that the Marines realized that the only people encountered on the approach were innocent civilians. They had fired on two young boys, teenage brothers. One of the boys was gravely injured, with four abdominal wounds. As the platoon medic examined the boys, he told Fick that it was clear that the wounds were caused by Marine ammunition. He also tells him that the boy needs immediate medical attention or he will die. The whole operation was based on bad intelligence, and now a moral and ethical problem had developed.

- ○ **You are now in the combat boots of Lieutenant Fick. What do you think should be done?**
- ○ **What do you think Doc Bryan is feeling at this time?**
- ○ **How might Fick's actions, regardless of his decision, be judged by his Marines?**

Doc Bryan requested that Fick contact the Battalion Surgeon and request an urgent medical evacuation. Fisk went to the Battalion Headquarters and told the Captain who was present about the situation. The Captain said the matter was above his level and he was not authorized to take action. The Battalion Executive Officer, second in command, was nearby, and Fick made the request to him. He was denied. The Major informed Fick that the Battalion Commander, a Lieutenant Colonel, was asleep and that he did not intend to wake him. He added that he was not going to endanger American lives to evacuate the boys, and told Fick to "deal with it". Now Fick becomes involved in his own challenge of leadership. He is angry, and even thinks of pointing a weapon at the Major and having him order the evacuation. He wisely decides to back off, but is now terribly angry and conflicted. Fick makes his way back to his platoon, and considers that ". . . our values have been inverted." Fick now locates the Battalion Surgeon and informs him of the situation. Under the rules of engagement, if a US Medical officer were to take control of the casualties, then there existed a moral and ethical requirement for treatment. The Surgeon and Doc Bryan found eight stretcher bearers and left for the Battalion Headquarters.

There they laid the stretchers down in front of the Major's tent. Doc Bryan, a Navy Corpsman, said "Here you go sir. You want to let them die, they can die right here in front of your tent." The Major was speechless. He was also faced with a real leadership challenge of his own. His subordinates had neatly placed him into the problem, and he had no choice now but to react in their favor. The boys were evacuated, accompanied by Doc Bryan.

- **What happened here?**
- **Was it what you expected from a military environment?**
- **Why and how did it happen?**

The boys were evacuated. But for Fick, the event was still very troubling from a leadership perspective.

- **Is this incident sufficiently resolved, in your opinion? Did Fick perform as a leader should have?**

Fick did not consider the incident resolved. He felt that as a leader, he should have made an attempt to countermand the free fire zone order from the beginning. He faulted his own decision in failing to countermand the order. His remarks to the platoon after Doc Bryan returned were revealing. In his own words Fick recalled: "Fellas, today was f—d-up, completely insane. But we can't control the missions we get, only how we execute them. I failed you this morning by allowing that declared hostile call to stand. My failure put you in an impossible position. First, we made a mistake this morning. Second, I need you to compartmentalize today. Third, no second guessing and armchair quarterbacking."[28]

Fick understood the burden of leadership, and struggled with emotion after he addressed his platoon. He realized that leadership had changed him, and with it came the loneliness of command.

Another very important issue in this event was the moral courage of Doc Bryan. He understood and accepted a personal obligation in his duty as a Corpsman. His insistence and action toward the Major was a fundamental reason for the outcome.

LISTENING POWER

"If you make listening and observation your occupation you will gain much more than you can by talk."

Robert Baden-Powell

CASE OBJECTIVES

- To learn to apply the basic element of communication and learn how it assists in the achievement of mission objectives
- To teach new leaders one method of how to relate to the human side of their followers

CONTEXT

A Navy Officer is serving as Commander of a small, specialized training group of the U.S. Navy. When he assumed command, the group was already performing at a very high level, and the last few percentage points of possible improvement would be difficult to achieve. The group had been well-led, and they tended to have a high education level. Many were either pursuing college degrees or had some experience past high school. All were specialists in their respective fields, and all had attended the Navy course which certified instructors for Navy schools.

As often happens in leadership, the key to unit improvement was delivered by one of the sailors. One afternoon a young petty officer came into the Commanders office and asked if he had some time to speak privately with him. He signaled for him to close the door, and for others to leave. For the better part of an hour he told him of his personal difficulties. When he finished he thanked the CO. He quietly passed the word that anyone who needed the CO's ear just had to let him know. Most people are not aware that among all of the specific duties of a Navy Commanding Officer, he is also tasked formally with the morale of his team. This is actually written into the ship's organization table as a line item.

- ○ **Leaders vote with their time. How must it be allocated?**
- ○ **Discuss the importance of morale in a team**

Over the next year or so he mostly listened to a series of personal issues. He rarely tried to give advice, but after each of his sailors left, they thanked him graciously for the simple act of listening. What he learned from that experience was that among this group, few had anyone whom would simply listen in a non-judgmental and non-critical manner. He rarely gave advice in these sessions, but usually asked questions and encouraged them to talk. The great surprise was to see them leave the office smiling and thanking him for what he perceived as a small investment of time.

During the time of the listening sessions he was able to see evidence of increased morale, especially among those to whom he had listened. While he doubted that this practice could account for measurable performance increases, he was certainly able to see an improvement in cohesion and sense of community. With morale, a leader can do almost anything. One of the very first items on the checklist of the new leader is to assess the morale of his team. Maintaining communication helps to bring about the power of the learning organization. While it may not always be a good idea to invite discussion of every personal issue, what is important is that issues regarding the organization and its performance should always be welcomed by leaders. You will be surprised to discover that the answers to most of the problems faced by a group, especially regarding operations, are to be found by the people you lead.

PLANE IN THE WATER!

"Reason and calm judgment, the qualities specially belonging to a leader."

Tacitus

CASE OBJECTIVES

- To place the proper value on calm and rational actions when under pressure
- To understand that calm contributes to performance and confidence

CONTEXT

As a requirement for qualifying as an Officer of the Deck aboard a Navy ship at sea, it is necessary to serve under the guidance of a senior qualified officer so that your competence and response under pressure can be observed. During one such watch aboard an aircraft carrier, the Junior Officer of the Deck (JOOD) was responsible for the conduct and performance of the watch team of several persons. On that watch, the first aircraft launched had a catapult failure and went over the deck. In such an event, it is important that several things happen at once. Plotters must mark the datum, or location in which the crash occurred. Ships in company must maneuver to avoid the aircraft if it is still floating. Markers must immediately be placed on the surface. Boats must be launched for recovery. The ship must maneuver to remain in the same area. Radio and internal communication messages must go out immediately to the force. All of this must be done quickly and well. Lives are at stake. Training is the key to success in such maneuvers, but there is another factor. In these events it is important to remain calm and to manage emotions and anxieties. If the person responsible for the team becomes panicked, the entire team may lose their poise and mistakes will ensue. The team was well prepared. Though they had never experienced a crash before, they had planned and practiced the procedures many times. Everyone knew their tasks. When it happened, they reacted exactly as they had trained. The officer of the deck was a very calm senior officer who never raised his voice. He really did not need to say anything except "plane in the water". After that the team began the work of responding.

- ○ **How does the organization for which you work respond to pressure?**
- ○ **How do you respond to pressure in a leadership role?**
- ○ **Are you as calm in a tense situation as this officer described his superior?**
- ○ **How does calmness affect performance?**
- ○ **Discuss the role of training in this instance.**

The JOOD was responsible for supervising the individual tasks of the team and when the watch was over, to write the log and detail the event for the record. He was in the process of doing this as the officer of the deck came over. "First time you've seen someone die?" he asked. "Yes" the JOOD replied. "You did well" he said, and gave him a tap on the shoulder as he left the bridge. That quiet confidence meant a great deal to those faced with the urgency of the crisis. It enabled each of them to concentrate on the tasks they needed to perform without more external influence than already existed. The OOD had overseen their training, and he was confident that his team would perform. Calm produces more calm, confidence produces more confidence. Training develops and enables both calm and confidence.

ROBERT E. LEE IN CHURCH

"A return to first principles in a republic is sometimes caused by the simple virtues of one man. His good example has such an influence that the good men strive to imitate him, and the wicked are ashamed to lead a life so contrary to his example."

Niccolo Machiavelli

CASE OBJECTIVES

- ○ To demonstrate the remarkable power and value of a single moment in the life of a leader
- ○ To show the importance of seizing leadership opportunities and the "moments" of leadership which present themselves

CONTEXT

General Robert E. Lee was a heroic figure in the American Civil War. After the war years, Lee returned to Virginia and became President of Washington College, which was renamed after his death as Washington & Lee.

As Lee was attending an Episcopal Church post-war, the time came for the communion service. A black man approached the rail and knelt to receive communion. At that time in America, blacks and whites had segregated churches, and the remaining members of the congregation were stunned by what they perceived as an affront. No one rose to walk forward and kneel. Lee understood immediately, and he rose, walked to the rail, and knelt by the black man. The entire congregation followed suit.[29]

- ○ **Describe what happened and why?**
- ○ **Is Charisma involved?**

- ○ **Courage?**
- ○ **Morality?**

Breaking old and established traditions requires significant moral courage. Lee's simple but forceful example motivated an entire congregation to change a long standing social practice. This single, small act by one man began the process of changing a culture. Robert E. Lee, in a single shining instant, bestowed the gift of moral courage. Lee's vision extended far beyond that event. He understood the change necessary to bring the South back into the Union and was prepared to lead by example.

SAMPLING THE CREW'S MESS

"Leadership comes in small acts as well as bold strokes."
Carly Fiorina

CASE OBJECTIVES

- ○ Provide an example of how an apparently transactional requirement can contribute to transformational leadership

CONTEXT

"Meals served in the general mess shall be sampled regularly by an officer detailed by the commanding officer for that purpose. Should he or she find the quality or quantity of the food unsatisfactory, or should any member of the mess object to the quality or quantity of the food, the commanding officer should be notified and shall take appropriate action."

US NAVY REGULATIONS, ARTICLE 1158

- ○ **Discuss how the transactional and structure works in this case to supplement transformational leadership. How might a leader apply a similar structure in a business environment?**

Food and the quality of food becomes a very important component of morale in the military. Aboard a ship it becomes even more important since the crew has no other place to eat. The practice of sampling the crew's mess is a structural acknowledgement that the morale and welfare of the crew is important enough to make a permanent regulation to see that it is attended to. On some ships this duty fell to the oncoming watch officer. Many ships provide a table for him in the mess area, and often on large ships he is instructed to wait in line with the rest of the crew. This was to ensure that he knows how long it was taking to serve. A form is usually provided at the table set aside for the officer sampling the mess. It detailed which items he was to inspect, including the heat of the coffee, the coldness of the iced tea, and temperature of the food items, the length of the line, and other issues. The form is turned in to the Executive Officer and each evening at Eight O'clock reports, it is presented to an assembled group of Department Heads. This is an example of a transactional structure designed to assist in transformational leadership.

TALKING TO THE ADMIRAL

"Leadership is a matter of intelligence, trustworthiness, humaneness, courage and sternness"

Sun Tzu

CASE OBJECTIVE

- ○ Demonstrate the need for clear and explicit limits on personnel authority when political or other external pressure is brought to bear

CONTEXT

It was a beautiful clear day in Southern California. I was standing watch as the Officer of the Deck-In Port. It was a Saturday, the ship was not likely to be getting underway at any time soon, and I felt sure that the watch was going to be quiet and without incident. The phone rang, and as the Quartermaster of the Watch listened, his face became serious. He motioned for me to come over, and holding his hand over the receiver, said "It's from the Command Duty Officer at Commander Naval Air Forces Pacific." Since we were an aircraft carrier, this phone call was from our highest local level of authority. The Command Duty Officer remarked that there would be a group of Congressmen visiting the ship next week. The ship had moored port side to pier. This was not the usual for carriers, but necessary because we needed some work done that was easier in this arrangement. Mooring in this manner required that the usual access was lengthened, and visitors and crew had to come aboard via a series of small floating barges linked together. The Command Duty Officer ordered me to find our Captain (this was long before cell phones) and tell him that the ship needed to be moved to a starboard to pier mooring arrangement so that the Congressional tour would not be inconvenienced. When a Command Duty Officer on the staff of your operating superior orders something, you assume that it is an order sanctioned by the Admiral. I hung up, and began trying to call our Captain at his home. Re-positioning our ship would require a pilot, tugboats, and manning a full crew for the operation. It would have taken several hours.

Two hours went by with no success, and the phone rang. The Quartermaster whispered to me "It's the ADMIRAL". I took the phone and began to explain to the Admiral that I had been unsuccessful in contacting our Captain, but was going to continue to try to reach him. The Admiral listened, and then chuckled. "Son, you just forget about that order. I would rather tell the President to go to hell than tell Jack Christiansen to move his ship so a bunch of Congressmen didn't have the inconvenience of walking across the barges. If it is good enough for our sailors, it is good enough for them." I thanked the Admiral and took a deep breath, relieved that I would not have to deliver the news to the CO.

Leaders at high levels often have to be aware that some followers exhibit a vicarious use of their leader's authority. Smart leaders understand that this is a possibility, and are able to prevent such shenanigans. It is likely that the Command Duty Officer received a markdown in his efficiency report in the category of "judgment". His desire to please his superior led him to be somewhat reckless in assuming that the Admiral would back his decision. As a leader, it is important to deliver a vision to your people. As a follower, it is important that you have enough ability to realize the scope and limits of that vision and act in accordance with it. Failure to do so can have serious consequences.

THE SS QUALIFICATION BOOK

"Trust is the lubrication that makes it possible for organizations to work."

Warren G. Bennis

CASE OBJECTIVES

- To demonstrate the use of structure as a tool in building cohesion and trust

CONTEXT

In the United States Navy Submarine Service, each crew member must go through a series of physical and mental qualifications prior to being assigned to an operating submarine. Once aboard, the crew member must then work his way through a qualification book in which he must demonstrate proficiency in each of the operating systems and equipment on the "boat" as submarines are called. This requires him to seek the signature and sign-off of each of the specialists responsible for the various equipment and systems, and to demonstrate to them that he not only understands the functions of the items, but is able to operate the equipment to the satisfaction of the requested signer. Thus it occurs that he might be seeking the signature of the Weapons Officer one day, and a signoff from the cook on the proper operation of the garbage ejection system the next.

Discuss the use of the qualification system. How does it affect the trust and cohesion of the group?

Does the sign-off process seem unusual for a military system? Why?

What are some of the purposes and outcomes of the system other than those which regard technical competence?

Discuss the transactional and transformational components of the sign-off process.

In this system, a junior officer will often find himself under the tutelage of an enlisted specialist who must approve his work and who has the power of admitting him into the ship's company as a trusted member. This system has been in operation for decades with little change. The qualification book system is much more than the "getting acquainted" approach which passes for training in many industrial environments. Commanding Officers of submarines will inquire occasionally ask enlisted men their opinions of the officers seeking signoffs from them, and inquire whether or not the officer is technically competent and displays confidence in mastering the systems.

In the words of one Captain, ". . . a submarine is a collection of pipes. Some of the pipes are for people, and some for water. Our objective is to keep the water out of the people pipe." The primary purpose of the qualification book is the achievement and progress of the person seeking membership in the community of the submarine service. But there is a deeper and greater process involved. Keeping the water out of the people pipe is a technically complex and demanding process. Any single event badly performed can mean disaster for the entire crew. The signing of the qualification book by an enlisted man gives him a chance to examine the officer's competence, and to determine whether or not he trusts the officer enough to admit him as a valued member of the ship's company. In this use of a structured qualification process, trust is one of the results. Having a formal written record for qualification is a valuable asset in any organization. As a team leader, it is important that you understand the issues involving trust, and determine how you might use a similar system to build trust and confidence in your own organization. In this matter it is necessary to examine whether you have developed trust in your followers, and whether or not your team has trust among its members.

THE YEOMAN'S EVALUATION

"There is always hope when people are forced to listen to both sides"

John Stuart Mill

CASE OBJECTIVES

- ○ To teach the new leader the importance of their involvement in the personal development of their followers

CONTEXT

A young Naval Officer assumes his first leadership role as the Division Officer of the Navigation Department on an aircraft carrier. In his capacity as Division Officer, he supervises about 35 people. His first task is to write a performance evaluation for the Department Yeoman. In the Navy, the Yeoman serves as the unit clerk, responsible for the written communications of the Department. He prepares what he believes to be an accurate evaluation for the young clerk, who himself has only been in the Navy for about one year, and submits it to his Department head for approval.

A few days later he is called to discuss the evaluation with his Department Head, who is not satisfied with the report.

- ○ **Discuss some possible reasons why the Department Head may not be satisfied with the report.**

The Department Head tells the junior officer that he believes the report is too critical. He also reveals that he does not think the junior officer is interested in the development of the Yeoman's skills.

- ○ **What type of organization culture does the Department Head believe the young officer is displaying?**

How might the young officer resolve the issue with his Department Head?

The Department Head believed that the Lieutenant needed to be less critical (transactional). He also wanted him to lead in the development of the Yeoman's skills by recommending a course of action that might improve the skills of the Yeoman. These might be correspondence courses offered by the Navy, or by sending him to an advanced course in the Yeoman rating offered ashore, or by the Lieutenant working personally with the Yeoman each time he felt coaching and improvement was indicated. In essence, he wanted the Lieutenant to be *invested* in the success of the Yeoman. He wanted the Lieutenant to be able to say that he had done everything possible to ensure the success of his follower. It was a brief but succinct lesson in leadership that emphasized the pulling, not pushing, exercised by true leaders. Together, the two would combine efforts to improve the chances for success, and both would enjoy the product of their efforts. Is it possible to be successful without someone you have trained to succeed you? Is it possible to be successful without successors? It may be possible but it is an indication that you have probably ignored the development of your team and failed to prepare them for greater responsibility. One of the factors in the evaluation of military leaders is whether or not their personnel are being promoted and retained *in the services. Failure to succeed in this task is an indicator of poor leadership.*

THE ZONE INSPECTION

> "There is no type of human endeavor where it is so important that the leader understands all phases of his job as that of the profession of arms".
>
> **Major General James Fry**

CASE OBJECTIVES

- To provide an example of how a structure designed around the transactional can evolve into a transformational opportunity

CONTEXT

In order to provide safe working conditions and maintenance of critical equipment, the US Navy regularly conducts what are known as Zone Inspections. Officers and senior enlisted are assigned spaces to inspect, and these are typically in areas where the inspectors do not work. The Zone Inspection has multiple objectives. Safety and upkeep are two. Familiarization of the inspectors with different areas of the ship is another. Having a different set of eyes inspect the area for which you are responsible provides a fresh view of your efforts and avoids bias.

A young Lieutenant from the Communications Department is assigned a zone in the engineering spaces consisting of two boilers and the associated control room. The decks and boilers are viewed to be in good condition, clean, free of grime and excessive grease and fuel oil. The control room is orderly, the intercommunication equipment works well, and the necessary manuals and safety directives are displayed properly. The young officer is about to conclude his inspection and award a high evaluation to the area when he notices a ladder going to the top of the control room space. There seems to be little reason for the ladder, and he becomes curious, since the space between the top of the control room and the overhead is only a few feet. "What's up there?" he asks the sailor in charge of the space; "Oh, nothing sir, just some space." Increased curiosity is the result. Ascending the ladder and looking out over the top of the control room, he discovers a large pile of oily rags stowed under a fuel line. This is definitely a fire hazard. He looks out over the scene for several seconds, pondering his options. The space is exceptionally well kept with the exception of the rag storage. He has inspected many areas before, and he is confident that the sailor in charge is proud of his space and keeps it well maintained, but the rags are a safety violation. He has a choice of writing up the young sailor for a safety violation, or some other possible action.

- **You are conducting the zone inspection. What is your decision?**
- **What should the transactional response be?**
- **Can you think of a transformational response?**

Descending the ladder, he tells the sailor that he really needs a cup of coffee, and that he will return to finish the inspection in about twenty minutes. He returns to find the space above the control cleared of the rags, and assigns a high score to the zone. He returns several days later to the space and again makes the trip up the ladder. The space is clear.

The purpose of the zone inspection in a purely transactional environment is to find fault and record it. The deeper and underlying objective is to change culture and unsafe habits. There is a necessary link between the transactional and transformational ends of the spectrum. In this case, the young officer felt that the sailor in charge of the space simply had a bad habit, probably passed on from earlier sailors in charge of the compartment. He was interested in changing habits more than punitive action. This was a judgment call. Sometimes judgment is not black and white, but shades of gray.

- ○ Discuss the actions of the zone inspector. Discuss possible variations of the decision he made.
- ○ Would you have done the same? Does it depend on the individual being inspected and the inspector?
- ○ Discuss the possibility of the evaluator going to the officer in charge of the area after the inspection and revealing to him the results. Do you prefer this in addition to what the evaluator did in speaking to the sailor only?

FIGHTER PILOTS AND OODA LOOPS

"Example is the school of mankind, and they will learn at no other."

Edmund Burke

CASE OBJECTIVES

- To instruct the leader that there is a need for constant assessment of the morale and productivity
- To provide a tool for use in a leadership plan

CONTEXT

Modern day fighter planes call for lightning quick reflexes and quick decisions. To perform in this environment military aviators employ a tool called the "OODA Loop".[30] The acronym stands for Observe, Orient, Decide, and Act. The idea of the loop was to speed up the operational tempo for the pilot, and to delay the loop cycle in his opponent. Simply stated, in the combat scenario, it is most desirable to keep your opponent in the "observe and orient" cycle as long as possible. In the environment of the combat aviator, this tool is used constantly and the consequences are dire in the event of failure. Fortunately for us in the business climate, we need not employ the tool in quite the same manner, nor do we have to worry about the same consequences of failure to act properly or rapidly enough. It is correct though to assume the same sequence and apply it to business decisions. Note that the final verb is to act. The operational tempo for a business leader is less rapid, but it is still a dynamic situation, and when leading people, every single interaction is subject to the rigors of the OODA loop.

The observation portion seems simple. It is very important to recognize that at this point, all we know about the situation is defined as simple data. Something has happened, and it has secured our attention. We have only raw facts, the results of observations, and it is insufficient material on which to act.

Now we need to filter that data, the facts, and attempt to make sensible information out of that collection of data. It's not yet what we could call information, or "informed data". But in this cycle, we are hindered and sometimes hampered by our own biases. We bring to our observations a set of prejudices caused by our own experiences, world-views, culture, and education. This analysis is part of the orientation cycle. It's where we filter the data, and make certain assumptions.

- **Do you know and understand enough of the tempo of operations in your organization to establish a frequency of observation?**
- **Do you further understand the critical events in the task processes of your organization; i.e. which events have priority?**
- **Do you have adequate situational awareness of the events within your group? Are you aware of the daily events impacting your followers and their performance?**
- **Can you define the areas of interest in your group?**

UTILIZING THE LOOP IN FORMING A LEADERSHIP PLAN

As leaders, we need to establish a consistent pattern of observing, orienting, deciding, and acting. Depending on the tempo of our operating cycle, this pattern can range from infrequent to nearly constant. Transactional institutions such as Departments of Motor Vehicles have a rigid and very predictable time-based pattern for their operations such as license renewals and inspections. Some leadership positions call for such rigidity, especially in procedure based organizations such as those, but more often as activities and goals and objectives change, the frequency of the OODA loop needs constant adjustment and change. Transformational leaders in particular must operate from variable time constants. They are concerned not with things, but with people and their interactions with each other. Morale and cohesion are ever changing and infinitely variable. Curiosity and continuous learning are mandatory for those who want to lead. Leadership is a destination, and we never fully arrive there. Curiosity and continuous learning ensure that we are always observing, orienting, deciding and acting. If we fail to do this, we are overcome by events. (OBE) To avoid OBE, it is useful to establish a frequency of occurrence for our OODA loops. This is where the transactional and structure aid and support the transformational.

We can formulate a broad type of leader plan from the OODA Loop. For a proactive leader, the loop is always in motion. Leaders continually observe, evaluate, decide and act. These processes must become a standard practice for leaders. The tempo of operations, changing technology, and group dynamics gives the leader a basis for loop frequency. In certain high technology environments it becomes extremely important to assess external influences acting on the group. The external environment acts with greater impact on some groups as opposed to others. It's one of the jobs of a leader to know and assess effects of the environment and the time constant that affects both his group and the larger organization.

THE ROLE OF CURIOSITY

Asking *why* things are done in a certain way is a good technique for leaders to begin the loop processes. Leaders above all must have a certain amount of curiosity as they approach challenges. In the Toyota manufacturing process, evaluation is performed weekly, and even low level employees are able to question and suggest in the Toyota model. Leaders who ask *why* will sometimes find resistance and defensive behavior. "We've always done it that way" is a frequent response. But until the issues are subjected to analysis, you will never know if the action or behavior is appropriate. The loop process and the leadership plan are appropriate for analysis of both interpersonal relations and mechanical processes. Leaders need to be proficient at both, but the leadership capital is always gained through people. People are the currency of leaders.

From the previous discussion, it should be evident that one of the important issues for a leader is determining the operational tempo and adjusting to it. It is important for all leaders, but especially so for new leaders. The new leader is faced with what sometimes is a necessity for quick action. The only way for this to occur is through a cycle of frequent observation. Later, once the actions desired are put in place, it is possible to reduce the frequency of observation. But the new leader has to immerse himself in the tasks and operations of the group in order to plan the next actions.

Working with a large trucking company in attempts to reduce accidents, a team introduced a training method called "commentary driving". Commentary driving is an established process for motivating drivers to assess the decision process in daily work cycles. It consists of a trainee riding with an instructor. The instructor asks the driver what he is observing as he drives down a street in various types of traffic situations. When drivers are asked to estimate how many times each minute they have to make a decision, invariably they will answer with a very small number. The instructor then tells them to do a simple commentary as they drive. The results are always surprising. In effect, we are asking for an audible description of an OODA loop. Drivers will typically be stunned as they realize how many observations they must make in a simple drive without even changing lanes or exiting or entering a freeway. Often the numbers approach 100 observations per minute.

While commentary driving is effective for simple task training, it has a greater usefulness when applied to organizational tempo. In today's fast moving organizational structures, leaders typically apply some method of analysis to their activities, but the OODA loop offers a possible quantitative tool which could prove useful for metric development and evaluation.

TWO HUNDRED BOX LUNCHES AND
TWO CASES OF SCOTCH

> "Wars may be fought with weapons, but they are won by men. It is the spirit of men who follow and of the man who leads that gains the victory."
>
> **George S. Patton**

CASE OBJECTIVES

- ○ To demonstrate the use and purpose of indulgence
- ○ To provide insight into the need for recognition and reward of all the members of an organization

CONTEXT

In January of 1969 the aircraft carrier on which I served returned from a long and arduous deployment to the war zone in Vietnam. We had had limited liberty in the usual ports, and our Captain wanted to do something to recognize the lower ranked sailors who had been cleaning, cooking, and painting for much of the cruise. He arranged for a special treat for these young sailors. They were to be the first off of the ship when we arrived in port. They would be given box lunches, and taken to two Navy transport planes which would then fly around the country and land at the nearest airport to their hometowns. They were also to be given uncharged leave, which would not be accounted for as long as they returned on time.

- ○ **What was the purpose of the Captain's actions?**
- ○ **What might the effects of such action be?**

It was his way of letting them know that even the lowest ranks had important jobs. He remarked that it had cost him two cases of very fine Scotch Whiskey delivered to the pilots and crew of the transports, but it would be worth it if his sailors understood that they were valued. This form of leadership is called indulgence, and the use of indulgence reaches far back into military history to the campaigns of Alexander the Great, when Alexander granted the newly married soldiers leave to be with their wives. The effect of the action of the Captain was twofold. It showed the enlisted men that their Commanding Officer recognized their efforts. But the effect it had on the officers of those men was a powerful example for them to follow. For the officers, it was a demonstration of how, later in their careers, they might see the opportunity to use indulgence.

HAVE YOU CHECKED THEIR FEET?

"You must love soldiers in order to understand them, and understand them in order to lead them."

Henri Turenne

CASE OBJECTIVES

○ To demonstrate the effectiveness of caring for the welfare of followers as a transformational element

CONTEXT

Colonel David Hackworth was a decorated US Army officer who served in World War II, Korea, and Vietnam. In his book "Steel My Soldiers Hearts" Hackworth discusses his efforts in rebuilding a demoralized and ineffective Infantry Battalion during his Vietnam years.

In the early phases of this attempt at recovering the efficiency and morale of the battalion Hackworth noted that each time his soldiers went on patrols for several days, he would lose a number of men on their return because of their feet being in such bad shape. Trekking for days in the humid jungles with wet feet created immersion foot, a condition found among infantry soldiers in such climates. Men were sometimes unable to recover in time to make the next patrol. Hackworth was concerned that the leaders of the patrols were not attentive to the problems of their soldier's welfare, and also concerned that efficiency was being lost.

○ **Which of the two concerns held by Hackworth is more important to the mission?**

Hackworth's concerns exemplify an Army motto "Mission first, people always". This means that while the mission is a transactional obligation, there are still opportunities to lead in a transformational manner.

- ○ **How might Hackworth reduce the incidents of trench foot while addressing the welfare of the individual soldiers?**
- ○ **What measures can he take to instill the proper attention to the soldiers' welfare in their Officers and NCO's?**

He put the word out that foot care was important, and began to limit the duration of his patrols so that the foot problems never quite developed before the patrol was ended. After one such patrol, Hackworth watched as the men returned. He saw a Sergeant ask the men to remove their boots, and he went along the line of men, touching the feet of each and observing their condition. In this case, the physical act of touch created an understanding among the soldiers that their leaders cared. We are not advocating the physical act of touching in all cases, only pointing out that in this circumstance it was a powerful symbol. But touching people in the abstract sense is an absolute requirement for leaders. This is particularly important in difficult jobs, where there may be physical hardship and sometimes danger. We create followers by motivating them, by psychological touch and caring. If we fail to do this, we do not create followers, only subordinates. "Mission first, people always."

- ○ **Do you, as a leader in your organization, understand adequately the conditions under which your people work? Have you actually *experienced* them in some fashion?**
- ○ **Have *your leaders* experienced them so that they may know your work conditions in detail?**

MANEUVERING AT HIGH SPEED

"To lead or attempt to lead without first having knowledge of self is foolhardy and sure to bring disaster and defeat."

Machiavelli, The Prince

CASE OBJECTIVES

- ○ To show the importance of knowing the situation fully before acting
- ○ To show the importance of delegation and trust in followers once given

CONTEXT

It is nighttime in the Pacific Ocean, and you are the Officer of the Deck aboard an aircraft carrier weighing 80,000 tons and racing through the rough ocean at more than thirty miles an hour. The Captain is asleep, and the ship is your responsibility. The weather is dreadful, with heavy wind, rain, and rough seas and very little visibility. The Carrier is the center of a formation, with two smaller destroyers to the left and right about 1000 yards away at a forty-five degree angle. The formation is proceeding through the weather at high speed. The night orders call for a planned turn to the left which will re-orient the formation so that one ship is directly ahead of the carrier and one to its right or beam. You take the radio in hand at the exact time called for in the night orders, and commence the turn. Both ships answer in the affirmative, and the turn begins. Suddenly, the ship on the right calls out that he has an emergency, and that his rudder is jammed in the full left position. This event is not something you can practice for. It is too dangerous. But you have several years experience, and know from that experience that the only safe maneuver is for the carrier to continue the turn until the destroyer on your right is clear of you.

At that moment, the Captain walks onto the bridge and overhears the exchange between you and the destroyer. He shouts for you to stop the turn. You know that this would place both ships in grave danger. The Captain has two options. He may relieve you immediately, in which case the responsibility for the event is totally in his hands. Or, he may continue to let you manage the situation. In either case, he will be responsible, no matter what the outcome. He does neither but continues to tell you to stop the turn.

- **What has happened here?**
- **Why? Is the OODA Loop at work here?**
- **What should the young officer do?**
- **What should the Captain do?**

There are other considerations too. As the Officer of the Deck, you have an immediate team of several people who work under your supervision while on the bridge watch. Your ability to lead may determine their actions as followers.

This Captain was a well-known "screamer". He was always on edge, and tended to act very quickly, which occasionally caused problems. The Officer of the Deck stood his ground, and refused the order. He did it by stating emphatically that he *could not* stop the turn. Note that he did not say "*I will not stop the turn.*" He knew from experience that keeping the rudder of the carrier full left would gain him some sea-room, and provide the destroyer time to bleed its speed off. He could not stop his ship quickly enough to avoid a collision, but keeping the rudder left would allow everyone in the formation some maneuvering space. His years of experience had taught him that the more nimble smaller ships would be able to maneuver more readily than he could. The Captain must have understood that the Officer of the Deck, though young, was standing his ground for a reason. Taking control of the ship at this time would have been wrong, because the Captain did not understand the situation well enough. After the incident, the ship's

Navigator took a maneuvering board and sketched the geometry of the event so that the Captain understood why the young officer acted as he did. The Captain never apologized for his outburst, but he realized that this was a very close call, and the matter passed without further comment. The team clearly saw the tension and the danger of the moment. They developed new confidence and trust in their team leader, and saw him display courage when it really mattered. The young officer knew that a collision at high speed, in darkness and rough seas, would likely cause the deaths of many of the destroyer crew.

- ○ **Compare this situation to your own work environment in terms of immediate decisions.**
- ○ **Do you face the same urgency in your daily work?**

One of the major lessons to be derived from this case is that when you enter a situation for the first time, without adequate knowledge, you have a good chance to make a mistake. Getting all of the facts fixed in your mind before acting is usually a good start. If you truly trust the people you have placed in positions of responsibility, as the Captain eventually trusted his OOD, you sometimes have to step back and let them make the tough decisions. The effect of this type of event is increased confidence in both the subordinate and the supervisor. It's an event that when handled successfully, acts to build morale and proficiency. If you intend to place people in positions of trust, it is your responsibility to be certain that they are ready to handle the position. You may delegate authority, but you may never delegate responsibility.

It's not always easy to know the difference between situations that call for immediate action on your part, and those that are often better left to someone else. But it is the job of the leader to know the difference. Leadership sometimes calls for risk. It's not pleasant, but it is part of the job.

RESPECT THESE (TEACH IN TANDEM WITH MANEUVERING AT HIGH SPEED)

"There is among the mass of individuals who carry rifles in war a great amount of ingenuity and efficiency. If men can talk naturally to their officers, the product of their resourcefulness becomes available to all."

General Dwight Eisenhower

CASE OBJECTIVES

- To demonstrate the confidence held by strong leaders when capable followers are given trust and responsibility
- To show the need for constructive critique and analysis from group members
- To demonstrate the need for collecting all points of view in a critical situation

CONTEXT

Before departing on one of our deployments to the Western Pacific during the Vietnam War, the ships Commanding Officer asked each of his appointed Officers of the Deck to meet with him in his in-port cabin. We were a young group, almost all in their early or middle twenties. Each of us had been tested and proven reliable. The Officer of the Deck is the direct representative of the Commanding Officer. He is responsible for the operation of the ship at all times, and especially when the Commanding Officer is not present on the bridge. It is a very important career achievement and sets the stage for even greater responsibilities. This Captain was an impressive leader. He had earned the Navy Cross in combat during World War II, and later earned a law degree and a Master's in International Relations. He would be promoted to Admiral at the end of his tour as our CO. He followed a previous Captain who was nervous and distrustful. We assembled as requested to hear what he had to say. He opened by telling us of our responsibilities and his trust in our abilities. Then he did something very unusual. Pointing to the silver eagles on his collar, he said, "Respect these but never fear them. The last thing I want around me is a bunch of "yes men". There will be times when you have a situation developing and you have worked out the best solution for it. You may have to wake me up at some dark hour, and I may well come out from sleep and tell you to do something really stupid. When that happens, I want you to challenge me, respectfully. Stand your ground and state your case. I may clear my head and come to my senses, or I may not. I want you to show courage and calm. That is the greatest thing you can do for me and for this ship and crew."

- Relate the events of this case to Case #8, "Skunks and Sycophants". Compare and contrast the two cases.
- Compare the actions of the two leaders in these cases to a typical leader in a civilian corporation. Is a true comparison possible?
- Discuss the need for confidence in leaders, and why and how confidence actually increases the potential for good decisions.

It should be clear to the reader that these cases do not represent the vision of the military as held in popular culture. Each of these events happened as described. Each presents a picture of the military that may seem foreign to the reader, especially one who has never served. Each event describes a behavioral situation acted upon by a leader. I was a participant in two of these. In reading through these cases, we see some common threads in each. Perhaps the most visible attribute of the leader in each of these cases is the trait of competence. Each of the leaders displayed the knowledge of the situation and the right manner of handling the problem before them. Each displayed a concern for the people they led, and each displayed a confidence that their actions would result in a predictable outcome. The effect of the leader's actions in each of these instances produced an increase in morale of their subordinates. Morale is one of the most important outcomes sought by a leader. Each of these events provided an opportunity for the leader to generate leadership capital, increase morale, and earn trust and confidence. In seeking to become leaders, you have to understand the opportunity as it presents itself before you, and to act accordingly. The second chance may not come for a long while, if ever.

CROSS TRAINING AND COHESION

> "Often in long periods of peace, mechanical thinking triumphs over the qualities of the heart and soul."
>
> **Scharnhorst**

CASE OBJECTIVES

- To demonstrate the need for challenge when morale and the tempo of operations dulls attention
- To apply a motivational challenge to closely knit and cohesive teams that strengthens the link between members and increases confidence

CONTEXT

There are times when your people become bored with their jobs. This can be dangerous. As an Officer of the Deck aboard an 80,000 ton, 1,000 foot long aircraft carrier, danger in some fashion was always lurking. As a young Lieutenant I was always concerned about this during the night and pre-dawn watches, especially when the ship was not engaged in flight operations, refueling or rearming. That was the time when bodies and minds began to experience fatigue and boredom. Sometimes the difference between success and failure is measured in seconds. There are several people on the bridge, each with a specific duty. Some are experts in navigation, radio, engineering, and other specialties. Each typically does only one type of function during the hours of the watch. I considered methods I might use to reduce the boredom during those watches where the activity level was low.

- **What does the mindset of the Lieutenant reveal?**
- **What suggestions do you have for him to reduce boredom and keep his team sharp?**

I wanted everyone on my team to be learning something, and when learning, they would tend to be as alert as possible. The more we knew and understood each other's jobs, the better we would perform as a team. My usual habit was to make a stop at the ship's bakery on these night watches and pick up a box of fresh donuts or cinnamon rolls for the team. This was always appreciated, since the team might not be able to eat for several more hours. The food was a sign that the team leader was interested in their welfare. (I liked the food too.) The team was composed of several officers and enlisted, and each of them had a specific and structured task. While we typically drilled to ensure competency in each task, we could only do so much of it before it became busy work, and the participants knew it. The goal is to understand the team well enough to know when they peaked, and when you might be overtraining. For the "slow" watches, I decided to cross train as many of my team as practical. It would keep the watches interesting, and sharpen the team skills. It was an intuitive decision, but once begun I learned more than I had believed. The cross training had other and more interesting effects, and turned out to be positive in more ways than I thought possible. If you are an 18 year-old kid from the Midwest whose biggest exposure to water was a stock pond, you might find steering a huge ship or operating a radio a great deal of fun. In the cross-training, we made sure that some of the enlisted got the chance to do some of the officer's roles too, ensuring they understood why we asked for certain tasks to be done in a specific manner. By broadening and deepening the team experience, morale was increased. Standing watch as a group is a true team experience, and cohesion was enhanced and sustained when each member learned and understood the roles of others. In the kind of environment in which we worked, speed and quick decisions were often critical. Members who understood that need through the actual experience were more likely to respond properly than those who did not. This type of training may not be as important in all civilian jobs, but in an example to be presented later, you will see how it can be applied in certain situations in the corporate world.

LUNCH WITH THE CHIEF

"The badge of rank (leaders wear) . . . is a symbol of servitude-servitude to soldiers."

General Maxwell Taylor

CASE OBJECTIVES

- ○ To teach the new leader the value of institutional knowledge
- ○ To enhance the respect of the new leader for followers
- ○ To teach the new leader the need to follow before leading and to build alliances among key followers

CONTEXT

The year is 1966. You are a young Naval Officer about to assume a leadership role for the first time. You are excited and ready to assume the new job. You are assigned to the Navigation Department of an Aircraft Carrier as Division Officer, and 30 sailors will be your responsibility. You report to the Department and meet the Department Head, learn where your sailors living quarters are located, and the duties of the Division Officer. You meet the Senior Petty Officers of the Division, enlisted men with as much as ten years of experience, and the equivalent of a senior Army Sergeant. After the initial welcoming and handshakes, one of the Chief Petty Officers asks you if you would like to join him for lunch off the ship at the Chief Petty Officers Club. You accept and the two of you leave the ship.

Over lunch at the club, the Chief asks you about your background, home, and generally gets to know you. Toward the end of lunch, he begins to tell you about each of the 30 sailors in the Division, their habits, work ethic, strengths and weaknesses. It's an amazing performance, as the Chief seems to have the personnel file of each of his men memorized. You are impressed. Then the Chief tells you firmly, but respectfully, that it would be best if for a time, you watched him and followed his lead. He asks you not to rush off and begin doing things on your own until you have both feet on the ground, and he and the Department Head are comfortable with you. You are somewhat taken aback. You had looked forward to assuming the leadership role on your own and proving yourself. The Chief seems to be telling you that he is in charge.

- What are the motives of the Chief Petty Officer in his lunch discussion with the young officer?
- Do you think the Department Head is aware of the Chief's action?
- What should be the response of the young officer?

The Chief was giving the Navy version of the "Sergeants Talk". He had a well running division. He had no intention of letting some new Lieutenant screw it up. He had been through the business of bringing up a junior officer before, and the Department Head knew exactly what the young officer and the Chief were going to discuss. The Chiefs and Sergeants of the military take great care in training young officers. They bring them into the system with dedication and focus. They teach them the basics of the system, and give them the perceptions of the soldiers and sailors from their point of view. They view the success of their officers as part of their own responsibility. This is an informal nurturing process, and present in all the militaries of the world. The military has been doing something similar to lunch at the Chief's Club for more than 200 years. They do it well. For his part, the Lieutenant was at least smart enough to keep his ego in check, and to realize that what he would learn from this man were the most important things before him. They developed a great working relationship, and there would come a time when the Lieutenant would have the opportunity to repay the Chief for his support. Getting caught up in the trappings of power is often perilous. Newly minted military officers must learn that the little gold bar on their collar has not made them a leader. They must earn that title. Spending time just talking calmly and without pressure is among the most important things we do as leaders. Learning from <u>everyone</u> around us is invaluable. To his credit the Lieutenant recognized the value of experience and was able to understand and accept that it was necessary to transcend rank. Leaders spend time with their people, and it is usually a learning experience for both of them. In addition to all of the formal training, and task specific training available in the military, the human factor still provides us with the most valuable element of leadership. That is simply to connect with those with whom we work in a productive manner.

COLONEL STRONG VINCENT AT GETTYSBURG

> "It seems to be a law of nature, inflexible and inexorable, that those who will not risk cannot win."
>
> **John Paul Jones**

CASE OBJECTIVES

- ◦ To illustrate the fact that sometimes urgency trumps protocol

CONTEXT

Colonel Strong Vincent, a twenty-six-year-old Brigade Commander in the Union Army, found himself in a very unusual situation on July 2, 1863[31]. A young lieutenant from the staff of the Commanding General was searching for the senior brigade commander with an urgent message. He had been sent to inform the commander to move his troops in position to block a confederate force moving toward the hill known as Little Round Top. But the messenger, confused and in the heat of battle, had been unable to find the senior officer when he wandered into Vincent's lines some distance away from the sought after commander. Vincent too was unsure of the exact position of the commander, and he asked the lieutenant what were his orders. The lieutenant informed Vincent that he carried a message for the commander, two levels of rank above Vincent, but had been unable to find him. He seemed reluctant to reveal the content of the orders to Col. Vincent.

- ◦ **Place yourself in Vincent's position. What is the most pressing matter before him?**
- ◦ **What might Vincent do about the messenger's predicament?**

Vincent did not wait or search for the senior Brigade Commander. He ordered the young lieutenant to give him the message meant for the General. He read the orders to make certain that he understood them fully. This was very bold because Vincent had now placed himself square in the middle of a communication meant for the commander of his immediate superior, two ranks above him. Vincent would be less remembered for this action than would Colonel Joshua Chamberlain of the 20th Maine Regiment. Chamberlain would become famous for his stand at Little Round Top. Vincent died only minutes after ordering Chamberlain's Regiment to hold the line. There are eminent military historians who believe that without the bold and quick action of Vincent, Gettysburg may have been lost. Retired General Colin Powell, in his list of leadership maxims, says that it is often easier to get forgiveness than to get permission. This is true especially in highly structured systems, like the Army. Col. Vincent did not have to ask for either, but he remains a fine example of boldness. He recognized that time was essential, and to waste it would diminish the opportunity that presented itself.

NO PURPLE HEART

> "The soldier's heart, the soldier's spirit, the soldier's soul, is everything. Unless the soldier's soul sustains him, he cannot prevail and will fail himself and his command and his country in the end.
>
> **General Maxwell Taylor**

CASE OBJECTIVES

○ To challenge the new leader to respect the contributions of his followers and value them appropriately

CASE OBJECTIVES

An Infantry Company Commander in Normandy during WWII related this story. It had been raining for some time and the regimental positions were in a thick muddy area. At some point he was summoned to the Battalion Operations area for a meeting of company commanders. He set out in the heavy rain of water and exploding metal, and just as he began to run toward the command post he heard the unmistakable sound of a large incoming shell. Continuing to run, he was suddenly thrown forward into the mud, his helmet blown off his head. The shell had gone deep into the soft mud and exploded several feet underground. He had an immediate hearing loss and had probably suffered a concussion. He was examined by the battalion surgeon who told him that his injuries qualified him for a Purple Heart, but declined. Many years later, his nephew asked him why he declined the award. He remarked that he did not feel it would have been proper to accept an award for what he considered an insignificant injury. He elaborated that he had seen the loss of life, and terrible wounds suffered by his troops, and that he would be diminishing the award by accepting it because of what he considered a minor injury.

- How do this incident and the Company Commander's action in refusing the Purple Heart contribute to the transformational paradigm?

If awards and sanctions are to have meaning and import, then it is worth considering that there are conditions under which we must decide whether or not to accept or to grant them. This is only common sense, but it is a rule often violated, as we shall see in a civilian case with a different outcome.

THE LAST PATROL

> "Leadership in a democratic army means firmness, not harshness; understanding, not weakness; justice, not license; humaneness not intolerance; generosity, not selfishness; pride, not egotism."
>
> **General Omar Bradley**

CASE OBJECTIVES

- To illustrate the intensity which develops in a truly cohesive group
- To reveal the sense of responsibility which leaders acquire

CONTEXT

Anyone who has seen the film series "Band of Brothers" will remember the portrayal of Major Richard Winters. Winters was a consummate leader, revered by his men. As with all combat leaders, he developed a strong bond with his men. Just how strong this bond was is revealed by the outcome of an incident that occurred toward the end of the war. Colonel Robert Sink, the Battalion Commander of the 506 Parachute Infantry had ordered Winters to undertake a patrol across a river into German territory. The objective was to capture German prisoners in order to gather better intelligence on German strength and troop disposition. Winters gathered a squad and briefed them on the objective. They crossed the river at night, and assaulted a house containing a German infantry unit. They returned with two prisoners, who were unable to give them any information of value. They also lost a man. Winters felt the attempt was a needless sacrifice of life. The Battalion was committed to another patrol and satisfied with the efforts of Winters's team, and Sink told Winters to make another attempt to take prisoners. Winters was stunned by the order. He returned to the squad that crossed the river the night before and briefed them on the second attempt. Then Winters did something unusual. He told the group that they would go to bed, get a good rest, and then report to him in the morning that they had crossed the river but were unable to capture any prisoners.

This story of this incident is not meant to urge anyone to take liberties with direction or orders. What it is meant to illustrate is how close the bond of combat renders warriors. We will rarely face the life and death challenges faced in wartime by Winters and his soldiers. But it is an example of the meaning of relationships, their depth and intensity. Winters had been in combat since Normandy, and saw no future in the Army as he planned to leave military service after the war. He knew the personal risk in disobeying the orders of Col. Sink. But the kinship he felt for his troops overcame his fear of the consequences of disobeying the order.

- **What are your personal limits? How far would you go to save your job? Would you do something illegal, immoral, and unethical?**
- **How close do you feel with your followers?**

ASKING QUESTIONS IN THE RANKS
(TO BE DISCUSSED WITH COMMUNICATIONS
FROM CORPORATE TO THE FIELD)

"Where there is no vision, the people perish"

Proverbs 29:18

CASE OBJECTIVES

- To reveal the differences between certain structures which inhibit communication and others which encourage it
- To examine the need for establishing an early communication channel and not waiting until things become critical

CONTEXT

In one of the most interesting scenes from a documentary filmed during the Desert Storm conflict, General Norman Schwarzkopf leaves his entourage of officers behind and walks into a huge area filled with cots. He stops and questions a private about the food, the living conditions, and the mail. Later in the documentary, a reporter asks Schwarzkopf why he drills down to the level of a private to get an answer to seemingly mundane questions. Schwarzkopf replies that by the time reports reach him, they have been filtered too many times to be reliable. Schwarzkopf elaborates by saying something to the effect that "Privates don't lie to Generals".

- **If we asked the same question in a typical civilian setting, what might the answer be?**

Consider the following actual case. The Chairman of the Board of Directors of a British based company has heard of problems with a US Director and his interaction with US customers. He schedules a visit to the US division. He says he wants an open and candid discussion of problems. He has never visited the US before, and none of the US personnel have met him before. The Director of the US group is actually British, and based in England. He will not be present for the meeting.

- Do you expect the Chairman to receive the same type of candid and open conversation offered to General Schwarzkopf by the private?
- Why or why not?
- What part does structure play in communication? Does it affect communication in each of these cases?

The group the Chairman visited had no prior communication with him, thus they had very little trust in him, despite the fact that they had serious problems with the British Director. As a consequence, they exchanged virtually no information, and the Chairman went back to the company headquarters with no understanding of the problems in the US branch.

The lesson here is that if you are a high level leader in a typical civilian corporation, you must establish lines of communication from the beginning. People are very reluctant to discuss information that may cost them their positions with someone they do not know or trust. One visit in a civilian organization does not qualify as a true communications opportunity unless there has been a back-channel established before the visit. The culture of open and candid conversation must be a part of the organization and well established so that people do not hold back.

RECOVERY ELEMENT ONE—AD HOC TEAM BUILDING

> "If officers desire to have control over their commands, they must remain habitually with them, industriously attend to their instruction and comfort, and in battle lead them well."
>
> **General Thomas "Stonewall" Jackson,**
> **to his commanders, 1861**

CASE OBJECTIVES

- ○ To provide an example of "ad hoc" team building and the proficiency that military leaders display in such efforts
- ○ To illustrate the challenge of a cross cultural team effort

CONTEXT

Mission

In conjunction with the government of Germany, Recovery Element One conducts excavation operations in Oberhof, (Germany) VIC 48Q XD 436555 from 5 July 2002 to 10 August 2002 to achieve the fullest possible accounting of Americans unaccounted for as a result of worldwide conflicts.

Site Information

Possible P-51D crash in 1944. Site identified by deceased local witness. Investigated four times immediately following WWII. Site never located. Information linking site to unresolved WWII case.

Loss Information

Possible crashed aircraft was flying as a bomber escort. Aircraft was reported missing 11 September 1944. A local resident reported the site and subsequent remains of a supposed U.S. serviceman and buried in an isolated plot. A significant amount of wreckage was reported at the site.

The preceding operation order is copied exactly as it was written. An Army Captain and Sergeant First Class along with a PhD forensic anthropologist and a variety of team members including a medic, photographer, an Explosive Ordnance Disposal expert to handle any bombs or ammunition discovered, and several mortuary affairs specialists were tasked with examining the site, recovering remains if found, and preserving any evidence that would prove useful in identification of the remains. A German interpreter will be on hand to interview local citizens who have knowledge of the site and if possible any witnesses to the incident in 1944. Most of the team members are from the same command, but many have not worked together. Teams may be composed of members from any service and frequently are mixed. The medic on this team will be a US Air Force member. The team includes one female member.

They will work in conjunction with a local interpreter and will be assisted by several civilian volunteers. They will be in civilian clothes for the duration, stay in a local hotel, and be interviewed by local media interests including television and print media. Much of the work is physical, involving digging, screening dirt for remains, and plotting locations of findings. The days will be long and the mission must be completed by the date ending on the operation order. Language is a challenge. Some of the German volunteers do not speak English, other volunteers are Czech. The leader of the Czech group is the person who discovered the crash site and he speaks English. You will work in all weather conditions. You need the manpower that the volunteers will provide. You also need to instruct them in the proper forensic techniques and protocols that must be used. Since the site contains human remains, security is necessary. A German military team will provide overnight security from the time your team leaves the site until they return each day. The premise is daunting. Lead a team of military and civilian members, speaking three different languages, from three countries, most of whom have never met. Come together for a period of just a few weeks to search for the physical remains of a man who died nearly sixty years ago. Do it according to very precise specifications and in accordance with a strict protocol, and complete the mission within a specified time.

- **Approach this as a problem in mixed or "ad hoc" leadership. While you have led many Army teams, this is a mixed group of volunteers. What if any changes will you make to your military leadership style to accommodate this eclectic group? The challenge is to meet the mission requirements, effect a recovery of remains, and do it all in a fun but businesslike manner. Discuss all the considerations you must take into account to accomplish your mission.**

On 5 July, the volunteers met with the team leader and unloaded the truck with tools, surveying equipment and other items. The briefing for the team and volunteers was held the next day. Volunteers are not paid but had a room and one meal per day provided by the US military at the hotel serving as team headquarters. The case had attracted local attention, and a press release was provided for print and TV media asking for information from civilians who knew something about the site and the possible location of remains.

Over the next several weeks, the team of civilians, American, Czech, and German worked side by side with the military members of Recovery Element One in a remarkable example of an ad hoc group. The Army Captain and Sergeant First Class had been on many recoveries around the world in their tour with the MIA recovery teams. They understood leadership and how to build temporary but effective teams. At the end of the day, the teams met on the road above the site to debrief. They talked about the day's problems, the successes, and planned the next day together with their volunteers. Then they retired to the hotel for dinner and drinks, or a swim in the heated pool to relax sore muscles. This was a chance for social interaction on a personal level, and it served as an opportunity to further bond. Friendships were formed which still survive many years later. The leadership shown by the team leader and Sergeant were tremendous examples of the best the Army has to offer. Humor was generously applied, and the word spread in town that the group was special, despite the physical effort and painstaking detail required. Volunteers soon began to appear on the road to the crash site in numbers, and the team had to turn them away. Good leadership is contagious. The group became a textbook example of the Tuckman model of groups. They formed, stormed, "normed" and performed. Pictures show the group on the last day of work. There are smiles, and hugs, and a subdued sadness with the realization that the work is ended and the group must end with it. Some management theorists have even added a fifth phase to the Tuckman Model, called "mourning". Mourning is the typical reaction experienced when successful groups disband. For all of the team, it was a moving experience and heavy with emotion as they left the site for the last time. They had brought missing remains back home, and they were filled with pride and achievement.

This was ad hoc leadership at its finest. The two team leaders had many years of Army leadership behind them, and they brought a special quality to the temporary team which enabled them to make a successful recovery of remains and have a great experience despite dissimilar backgrounds and cultures. Following the Army slogan of "Mission First, People Always", they performed remarkably.

THE REINVENTING LICENSE

> "There is a soul to an army as well as to the individual man, and no general can accomplish the full work of the army unless he commands the soul of his men, as well as their bodies and legs."
>
> **William Tecumseh Sherman**

CASE OBJECTIVES

- Show how the military, despite its rigorous transactional structure, will develop a transformational mindset when the mission demands

CONTEXT

One of the most successful military adaptations of organizational structure is the composition and organization of Special Forces teams and other special operations groups in the military. Most often these teams are not led by the person senior in rank but rather with the requisite experience to bring about the result. This is a dramatic departure from the hierarchical structures of the past, but it has been proven many times, and most recently in Afghanistan. Often leadership presents as a paradox. One such paradox is the "Reinventing License" issued by General Wayne Downing when he served as the Commanding General of the US Special Operations Command. The Reinventing License was a wallet-sized card that asked the following;

Is it the right thing for our country? Our forces?

Is it consistent with our organization's values?

Is it legal and ethical?

Is it something you are willing to be accountable for?

If the answer is YES to all of these questions,

DON'T ASK PERMISSION, JUST DO IT!

- ○ **Can you envision any scenario in your current business that would allow for using such a concept as the Reinventing License?**
- ○ **What conditions would be necessary for you to create the use of such a concept?**
- ○ **Once created, how would you apply and control such a license?**

Most often these teams are not led by the person senior in rank but rather the person with the requisite experience to bring about the result. They must also assume the responsibility for any problems caused by the "reinvention". Paradoxical indeed, that an organization perceived to be so rule and procedure bound would have such a written statement by its senior executive. General Downing did not hand these out to every member of the SOC. But he did issue them to those in whom he had a special trust, whether they were a senior officer or enlisted. This kind of challenge frees up the initiative of people in the organization to improve without getting permission as they see the opportunities before them. That kind of improvement happens quickly, without debate or discussion and inspires people to actively seek out problems.

There are companies in private enterprise that have created such licenses. Some are created around the safety of dangerous processes such as drilling for oil or operating refineries. The holder of such a license is authorized to stop a process which he or she deems dangerous.

LEMAY´S FIRST MISSION

> "Duty is the sublimest word in the English language."
> **Robert E. Lee**

CASE OBJECTIVES

- ○ To illustrate the need for personal involvement in matters concerning new visions and procedural changes
- ○ To understand the value of presence

CONTEXT

Curtis Lemay was an Air Force General who is perhaps best known for his creation and leadership of the Strategic Air Command in the years after World War II. Lemay had begun his flying career in the 1920's and when WWII began, he was a lowly First Lieutenant. Four years later he was a Major General. There are many examples of his leadership, but this one stands out.

In November of 1942 Lemay was a Colonel in command of the 305th Bomb Group During training in England, he realized that planes rarely returned with photos that could be used to determine the damage inflicted on targets. Lemay realized that the planes were taking evasive action over the target, and they were not only missing targets, but had no record of the efforts and therefore no way to measure success or failure. Success, if it happened, was accidental. Lemay was a consummate student of airpower. He analyzed everything and knew the jobs of everyone in the command. He determined that the only way for daylight bombing to succeed was to commit to a tight, organized formation that stacked airplanes in a box from high to low with interlocking defensive fire. And, the group was to retain that formation over the target, no matter what. The formation would give the planes some protection from German fighters, and the "straight line" approach into the target would provide for a way to measure the performance of the bombers. Lemay delivered the news to the assembled crews in the predawn briefing. It was not well received. The crews felt it was suicidal to fly in an organized formation in a straight line. Lemay believed in his new tactic. A bold pilot stood up and told Lemay his thoughts on the idea. As the crews reacted negatively, Lemay quietly looked over the assembly and said in his soft voice, "I'll fly lead". It was the first combat mission of his career. The group realized that if he was willing to be in the first plane, then he must have believed in the idea enough to risk his life. They gathered their equipment and filed out to their waiting airplanes.

- ○ **Presence in crisis is an obvious quality of a charismatic and transforming leader. In addition to that, what is the other primary leadership quality demonstrated by Lemay?**

Among other things, leaders must always pursue truth. The 305th, and other groups in England, had not enjoyed success in bombing. Lemay was the first to analyze the root cause and find a solution. His curious and analytical nature provided the answer. Whether in war or business, leaders should never accept the truth as stated without probing and verifying. In war, the price is lives, but the need for probing and proving is just as necessary in business. Pursuing a problem past the immediate solution to its origin and cause is transformational.

CREW CARE—BARRACKS VS. DORMITORIES

"Perfect courage is to do without witnesses what one would be capable of doing with the world looking on."

Francois de La Rochefoucauld

CASE OBJECTIVES

○ To demonstrate the role of support required by leaders in the overall mission
○ To show the occasional need to break with procedural issues in order to achieve the mission

CONTEXT

The task of developing the mission and operation of the Strategic Air Command was given to General Curtis Lemay. Very little of the form and function of the old U.S. Army Air Forces remained in SAC after Lemay. One of the problems he faced was how to build an organization tasked with a 24-hour alert schedule. There were issues of aircraft maintenance, weather, communications, and a host of other challenges. Money was one of them. After WWII and Korea, the military was in a typical peacetime status. Money was scarce and appropriations were carefully scrutinized, sometimes taking months to decide on approval or disapproval. One of the issues that Lemay was grappling with was the alert schedule and its impact on crews. Traditional military housing for aircrew was the barracks. This posed a problem for Lemay because not all crews were on alert at the same time. There was a constant flow of crews coming on to and off of alert, and the barracks was not a restful place for men who needed to get their rest and be fully alert to fly at any time. Mission performance was compromised by the living conditions. He needed two things, new, different type housing, and money to build it.

- ○ **In Lemay's position, what options do you have? You must improve the living conditions, but have apparently few options.**

Lemay was not to be defeated on this issue. He clearly understood the impact that living conditions had on his crews. He also knew this was one of the times when he would have to "think outside of the box" and proceeded to do just that. Lemay had established Omaha as SAC headquarters. Instead of going the traditional route of military procurement, he started in Omaha, and took on the project as a personal initiative. He began to cultivate the businessmen of Omaha and acquaint them with the problem, approaching it as a community issue. As an engineer, he had a finely tuned understanding of projects and their management. The local businessmen assisted, even to the point of donating money and construction services. Lemay had the community build three demonstration barracks, and local citizens furnished them. Today, nearly all military barracks other than basic training quarters are constructed in the Lemay design. He had also been concerned with the quality of food served in military establishments. He reached out to the best known civilian restaurants, and sent Air Force cooks to serve an "internship" with them to improve food. All of these changes contributed to the morale of the SAC crews and the culture of the organization.

- ○ **Explore the options for creative problem solving as a transformative leadership quality in your own organization.**
- ○ **What are the cultural and administrative barriers to such thinking and actions?**

THE CASE FOR HUMOR

"You can turn painful situations around through laughter. If you can find humor in anything, even poverty, you can survive it."

Bill Cosby

CASE OBJECTIVES

∘ To demonstrate the value of humor and discuss its place in an organization

CONTEXT

The folklore of your organization consists of the verbal history of events that are reminiscent of its success, humorous events, and challenges met. It is more often referred to in terms of things such as sales victories or other corporate accomplishments that over time take on the shine of legends. In the military, this occupies a very strong place and is used often. The application of this is a good indicator of morale within the organization. I have a story of my own. After an evening of carousing in a Caribbean port, three of us, ships officers of a US submarine found ourselves without transportation as the sun arose. We needed to get back to the boat before quarters. As we began our walk back to the pier, which was several miles away, the streets were empty except for a lone garbage truck. We flagged him down and he offered to take us to the base, but the only room available was on the back bumper. We took it, and topside watch alerted the entire forward torpedo room as we clattered up to our berth on the pier, riding in splendor amid the fumes. We became part of the Atlantic Submarine Forces legend, although not a glorious part. I'm sure that even today, someone in the Submarine Force is telling that story with the objective of letting the listener know just how important it is to be there for the crew muster at 0700, no matter if you have to ride a garbage truck to be there. It's all part of the ethos and "feeling" that contributes to morale. Giving the men we worked among a chance to laugh at us was good for them and for us. A little humility of this type contributes to morale. Look for opportunities to create it if you don't have it. Humor is a powerful contributor to the satisfaction of the group. Use it when you can. A workplace where people laugh is usually productive.

- **On a scale from one to ten evaluate the level of humor apparent in your organization.**
- **Is there an organizational or professional constraint that limits humor in your group or is there an inhibition among members that limit it?**

HITLER, ALEXANDER THE GREAT, AND PRESENCE

> "Out of every 100 men, ten should not even be there. Eighty more are just targets. Nine are the real fighters, and we are lucky to have them, for they make the battle. Ah, but the one. One is a warrior, and he will bring the others back."
>
> **Heraclitus**

CASE OBJECTIVES

- ○ To highlight the differences between real and false presence
- ○ To demonstrate the limits of technology

CONTEXT

Alexander the Great, perhaps the greatest leader in history, had a compelling leadership style. Always at the head of the troops, he accumulated numerous wounds in his battles. He was perhaps one of the archetypes of the heroic leader, who led by example and shared experience. On one occasion, when his troops showed fear, Alexander stripped to show them his wounds, eight of them; so that they could better realize that he led from the front. In this way, he strongly established his kinship as one of their brothers-in-arms.

Adolph Hitler had in fact experienced war as a youth, and had served with distinction. He was a messenger, who carried written orders from Battalion Headquarters to companies at the front. He was wounded and spent five months in a hospital recovering. The experience as a messenger was to shape (and mis-shape) his concepts of warfare and leadership from 1939 to the war's end. During World War I it was customary for Generals and their Staffs to establish themselves far from the front in spacious and comfortable chateaus. Communication was difficult and risky, and carried out by runners such as Hitler. This vision of command was also to insert itself into his thought and was reflected during his tenure as Commander in World War II.

Hitler's Generals struggled continually with his belief that he knew the realities of the far flung campaigns in Russia, North Africa, Italy, and Normandy. His attitude developed in this manner because of the vast differences in technology. Now, as a Commander, he misunderstood the effect of the instruments of communication such as the radio and telegraph. In his memory, the function he served as a runner, going above ground and then to trenches to deliver messages was now obliterated by technology. Further, he believed that this technology delivered the full and complete picture to him though he was hundreds or even thousands of miles distant. Thus his Generals continually found themselves in conflict with him as he often made decisions based on a poor understanding of the true nature of the battle scene.

- **What is the risk that we assume regarding information when we embrace modern technology?**
- **How might shared experiences of leaders and followers contribute to the leadership paradigm?**
- **Discuss the role—pro and con of electronic mail in the work of leaders and followers. Does it represent reality or simply data?**
- **Place yourself in the role of a modern commander or CEO. Just how much information and at what speed can you effectively absorb such amounts of information?**
- **To what extent must a leader "see" the action?**

HOLD ON GENERAL!

> "A good plan violently executed now is better than a perfect plan executed next week."
>
> **George S. Patton**

CASE OBJECTIVES

- ◦ To understand the differences between planning and execution and their relative importance
- ◦ To demonstrate the importance of challenging strong leaders and the fact that there are some processes and procedures which are inviolable and have far-reaching consequences

CONTEXT

In his book "An Army at Dawn" author Rick Atkinson describes the frantic loading of troop transports and supply ships in preparation for an ocean crossing and eventual landing in North Africa.[32] One of the things Naval Officers learn is the importance of the "last in-first out" principle of loading amphibious ships. Patton, who was to be the overall commander in the invasion, used his overbearing personality to override Navy procedures and load as supplies were received. He said "we'll sort it out later" or words to that effect. I will admit that the above quote was probably meant to define the tempo of combat operations, but it is also true that Patton had little experience as a staff officer and probably a disdain for planning. The load planning is a very important process, and must be followed closely, otherwise soldiers find an abundance of things they don't yet need while searching fruitlessly for things they need desperately. Amphibious loading is one of the few places where the plan has to be nearly perfect, because the force is in need of many things during the critical first few hours and days. While the quote attributed must be fairly assessed as a reference to combat and maneuver, it also gives us insight into the personality of Patton.

Patton neither understood the importance of amphibious loading nor had the patience to learn. The result was the cause of many deaths and foreseeable difficulties. In this case, Navy leaders simply let Patton run with his impatience and dominating personality. In fairness to both services, the Pacific was the test arena for amphibious operations, and there was scarce amphibious experience in the Atlantic arena available to planners. Leaders need to be courageous enough to slug it out with overbearing personalities. It's that business of courage again.

- ○ **Does the above quote attributed to Patton give us an indication of how he might approach a process of planning?**
- ○ **Is the quote more applicable to combat or to planning?**
- ○ **Should the Navy Admiral have overridden Patton?**
- ○ **If not, what does this say about the Admiral and his leadership**?

A GENERAL IN THE TENT

> "I love the Corps for those intangible possessions that cannot be issued: pride, honor, integrity, and being able to carry on the traditions for generations of warriors past."
>
> **Cpl. Jeff Sornig, USMC;**
> **in Navy Times, November 1994**

CASE OBJECTIVES

- ○ To reinforce the requirement to assess morale frequently
- ○ To understand the values of group traditions, customs, and folklore

CONTEXT

This case was described by a Marine Private who witnessed it in 1957. It occurred during a large scale military operation in the Philippines called Beacon Hill. The PFC was sitting in a large tent during a break in the operation. He was listening to a group of older Marines talking about their experiences in the Corps and its history. The tent flap lifted, and a head poked in and began to crawl into the tent. The PFC recognized the face of General Victor Krulak, and as he prepared to call the group to attention, Krulak put his finger on his lips to alert the Marine that he wanted no recognition. Krulak entered, sat at the back of the tent for some time, and left as quietly as he came.

- ○ **What was General Krulak's objective?**

Krulak was looking for the survival and the persistence of Marine Corps traditions and lore. As he listened to the group, he heard stories of the history of the Marine Corps, its traditions, values, and spirit. He left feeling that the morale was being well nurtured and the legacies of the Corps were intact.

This method of listening continued when Krulak became Commander of the Marine Corps Education Center at Quantico. Krulak gave orders to instructors not to call the room to attention as they trained their Marines. He wanted to hear the truth from all sides.

Years later, his son Charles was named Commandant of the Corps. In a letter to Charles, he wrote; "The greatest contribution you have made and the best and the most valuable by far, is not even visible. Call it what you will-honesty, truthfulness, character, morality, reliability, integrity, dependability. Any one will do. In each and every case, it creates respect, and not just for you, but for the entire Marine Corps. That is one hell of a legacy to leave."[33]

CHANGE OF COMMAND

> "Management is efficiency in climbing the ladder of success; leadership determines whether the ladder is leaning against the right wall."
>
> **Stephen R Covey**

CASE OBJECTIVES

- ○ To introduce the new leader to the existence of a micro-culture within a larger culture
- ○ To demonstrate the importance of beginning a culture change immediately and forcefully upon assuming leadership

CONTEXT

Our US Navy ship had been in the combat zone conducting operations against North Vietnam in 1968. We were scheduled to have a change of command. The existing Captain was competent but very fearful of failure. He created an environment of a myriad of new rules and regulations, and inserted practices designed to protect him from the expected failure. Micromanagement became the standard. New reports in addition to the usual requirements of Navy Regulations were promulgated. There was even a "Report of Reports" signifying that we had complied with all reporting requirements. Morale dropped precipitously. We were still combat ready, but had lost some of the edge we typically possessed. His fear of failure was contagious.

- ○ **Compare and contrast this environment with your own business or education group. How might you go about changing such an environment?**
- ○ **What would the advantages be in a military versus a civilian environment? What significant differences are in play?**

Mid deployment, we had our change of command. The new Captain was as different from the previous one as he could possibly be. After the previous Captain left the ship, our new CO made an announcement. He told us that we had forgotten our mission. It was simply combat. Anything that deterred us from that mindset and mission was to be dismissed and discontinued. It was to be done immediately. His actual words were a bit more "salty" than that, but you probably can envision the situation.

It is necessary, when changing a pervasive and morale-sapping culture, to do it definitively, with great impact and forcefulness. The case on page 134, "Respect These" was the next event to occur in the cultural change. Military cultures in some respects are easier to change due to organizational structure and leader authority. But they are not immune to the micro-cultures which creep in, and they must be removed with significant impact and clear messages.

BUSINESS CASES

In the following cases, we will see examples with mixed results. Many will exhibit the results of missed opportunities, some will illustrate the use of transformational principles. Each is an actual event. Many of these will exhibit the application of both structure and communication in the business workplace.

BUILDING THE FOUNDATION—
A COMMUNICATION EXERCISE

> "The key to success is to get out into the store and listen to what the associates have to say."
>
> **Sam Walton**

CASE OBJECTIVES

- ○ To enable participants to distinguish between communication and information
- ○ To give participants a format for the establishment of an interpersonal and face-to-face communication plan to set the conditions necessary for leadership

CONTEXT

We discussed the requirement for the Transactional and Transformational to exist together. The transactional is not a new concept, just a new term for a very old concept. In this case it's important to examine some of the problems we face when the transactional is not in place or firmly established. We'll look at the problems that occur when this happens, and what to do about it.

It matters little whether or not you are a great or a poor leader or manager. Without communication, you cannot be great, and with it, even the poorest of leaders will occasionally be successful. In the simplest of transactional models, communication can be seen as telling someone what to do and when to do it. The reality of becoming an effective communicator is more difficult and sophisticated than that, but it can still be expressed in simple terms. In those terms, communication is the passage of truthful and essential information between persons. No more, no less, that's it. But how often does that happen? In good, cohesive groups and teams, it's the standard. They live by it. Data becomes information, and information becomes knowledge, and, sometimes, knowledge becomes wisdom.

Do not assume that because you are there and in the role of a leader that communication is occurring. It is an active and dynamic process. Communication requires that a leader continually oversee the process of communicating and seeking dialogue. I once had the commanding officer of my first ship tell me that one of the most important things I could do was to spend some time with my sailors, having a cup of coffee and talking. This was in addition to the regular and formal meetings we had as a part of Navy routine and tradition. Establishing a relaxed and informal line of communication takes down some of the barriers and allows people to speak to you on issues that are important to them.

When truth becomes a common currency in your organization, you have become a learning organization. How does a leader go about setting up a truthful exchange of information?

THE COMMUNICATION PLAN

Project managers know the value of a communication plan. It is routinely assessed as the single most important component of a project. The reason for that is simple. If you do not know what the problems are, you cannot possibly manage them. For project managers, the issue of time is essential. Often a project manager will inherit a team, a project, and a deadline all in a very short time frame. Under these conditions it is necessary to utilize structure to your advantage, and the project communications plan provides the keystone element of the necessary structure. It is extremely important for new and emerging managers to grasp this concept. Equally important is for these new manager-leaders to proactively pursue communication with superiors and subordinates alike. For a complex organization with time driven tasks, a formal communication map may be required. But among the formal plan requirements should be some time set aside for relaxed and informal communications. Once you have learned how to do this and gained the trust of your people, you will find that some of your greatest lessons come from the people you lead.

The communication plan can be simple or complex. It depends on the size of the organization and the place the leader occupies within the structure. In large manufacturing operations, just as in the military, communication often is required in real time and in several directions at once.

A labor or construction crew might need a simpler plan, perhaps a daily meeting at beginning and ending of shifts. No matter the complexity, the plan begins with the obvious. You, as a leader, are at the center of the plan. You need to devise a simple graphic and begin to list the various subordinates, clients and superiors with whom you must communicate, like spokes radiating outward from a wheel. In this example we will use the role of an area manager for a trucking company. This list is not intended to be comprehensive, but only a guide to provide a visual explanation of the concept. In this example, the area manager reports to the regional manager and the fleet and safety managers are staff managers with no direct reports. Drivers are the only direct reports to the area managers.

The various documents or meetings that comprise the communication map are listed numerically below the map, and referred to by each of their numbers. We will use the following list of communication events as examples:

1. **Driver observation reports**
2. **Weekly safety meetings**
3. **Key productivity indicator reports**
4. **Accident reports**
5. **Fleet maintenance bulletins**
6. **Daily pre and post trip inspection reports**

DISCUSSION

- ○ **Which of the following communication events listed above involve data and which involve face-to-face communication?**
- ○ **Depending on your job description and roles, do you find the above events supportive of transformational leadership? i.e. distinguish between the roles of upper to middle management and the on-scene group leader**

The next step is to build the communication map. In this example, we will state that items 1 and 2 are generated by the leader, or area manager. Item 3 is generated by the regional manager, item 5 is generated by the fleet manager, and item 6 is generated daily by each driver. The safety manager is responsible for generating item 4, although the preliminary format for this report is done by the area manager and submitted to the safety manager for distribution. Our completed communication map appears below;

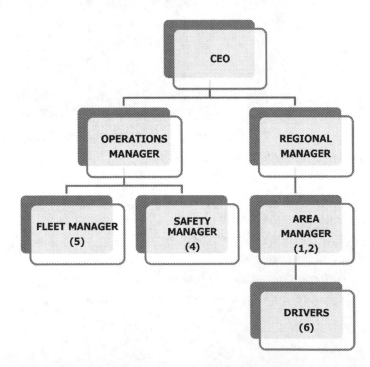

Now that we have an idea of the requirements for communication we can study just how much communication is required and what form it takes. As we look at the six items, we can learn something from their descriptions. The only items that require a significant face-to-face communication with the drivers in this list are items 1 and 2, the driver observation reports and the weekly safety meetings. The driver observation report is done as the manager rides in the truck with the driver once each month. The safety meeting requires the manager to meet once a week with their drivers and spend time talking about safety issues and other driver concerns. All the other items, 3 through 6, essentially fulfill transactional roles in the operation of the company. These items are important, and are required either by company rules or in the case of the vehicle pre and post-trip inspections, required by Transportation Regulations of the Federal Government. The communication map becomes a sort of an audit tool, telling us how frequently and in what directions we pass information and data. But it also tells us the nature of the communication. In this scenario, we can see that the only opportunities the area managers have to interact with their direct reports are their weekly safety meetings and the monthly driver observation.

Use the communication map as an analytical tool. You will often be surprised at the number and direction of the communication required of you. Often, the sheer numbers of communication events directed at and received from those whom you do not lead will detract from your role as a focal leader. You cannot relieve yourself of the transactional responsibilities to the organization by failing to perform these obligations. Becoming "O.B.E." or Overcome By Events is one of the ways that leaders fail in their primary responsibilities to those they hope to lead. Followers know and recognize this and once they see it, develop the perception that your loyalty is upward and not to them. A true transformational leader will balance both of the obligations. A transactional manager will address the obvious and measurable issues. It isn't easy, but it can be done.

You must also understand that communication and data are two distinctly different things. Corporations, especially to satisfy transactional metrics and often legal requirements, send huge amounts of data between groups. Some we do because it is necessary, others we do only because it is possible. Know the difference. Send the data asked of you, by all means. But find the time to transform by practicing true communication.

THE LONG MEETING—USING STRUCTURE

"The two words 'information' and 'communication' are often used interchangeably, but they signify quite different things. Information is giving out; communication is getting through."

Sydney J. Harris

CASE OBJECTIVES

○ To reveal the problems which develop through a lack of a structure for communication
○ To illustrate how the emotions of a pent-up group will exercise power

CONTEXT

This case builds on the data we reviewed previously in the communication map we constructed. The corporate safety manager has mandated a weekly ten-minute meeting involving safety, and provided training materials for you, the area manager to use. The safety manager is concerned with the accident rate, and believes that a brief weekly focus on safety will help drivers to reduce their accident rate. This is the first time that the company has held regular meetings for drivers. In the past, the drivers have been given their routes and left to their own devices. Most of them begin their routes late at night or very early in the morning, so you do not see them often. The materials are suitable, and the topics are pertinent to driving safety. You begin to hold the meetings as instructed, but the meetings last much longer than ten minutes. You talk to your counterparts in other areas, and they tell you that they are experiencing the same problems. They start out with the brief safety meetings, and then things expand to half an hour or longer, delaying the start of the drivers on their routes or keeping them longer after they are finished. You are concerned and irritated because the productivity of the drivers may be diminished. The drivers do not seem to be concerned however. They keep bringing up other issues not related to safety, but which they feel are important. You have some concerns. The performance indicator report is very detailed, and tracks driver hours and revenues. You want that number to continue in a positive direction, but the time taken in the meetings drives the number down. The drivers are also asking questions that require you to spend time in research. You really would like to get on with the business of running the area and just spend the ten minutes and be done with it. You had been requested to begin the monthly driver observations by riding along with the drivers, but you have not done that yet.

- **What motivation compels the drivers to stay beyond the ten minutes?**
- **What should you do about it?**
- **Is it necessary for you to be there personally to conduct the safety meetings? If so, why, and if not, justify your answer.**

Leaders have to become adept at determining root causes of certain issues, especially those involving human relations. At first glance, it seems that you could just extend the ten-minute meetings and consider the problem solved, and it might be. But that would ignore the heart of the issue. In this true to life case, the issue was a long standing disconnect between the drivers and their managers. The drivers had little contact with the manager, and their perception was that they did not count. The transactional requirement of the safety meeting revealed a problem, and pointed the way to a solution set.

Let's take a look at some approaches the managers might use to get to the root cause, and how they might work. The first observation is that there is a need for more frequent, honest communication between drivers and managers. That should be clear. The drivers have concerns and feel the need to voice them, even though it might detract from the completion of their routes or keep them after the routes have been completed. Just knowing that gets us a step further toward resolution. But that alone isn't enough. The managers need to know how to resolve the issues that are brought up by their drivers. In some cases, the issues are local and can be addressed locally. In others, the issues are the responsibility of corporate leadership. No matter where the responsibility lies for resolution, the organization as a whole will benefit from the attention given to the problems. This is a very basic issue, so simple that at first glance, it seems obvious. But as simple as this is, it is one of the most common problems, and is frequently overlooked. Going back to the communication map, we see that much of the communication is data that supports the transactional model. Good, we need that. It serves as our report card, gets us bonuses, pleases the stockholders and upper management. It's the fuel for the organization and without it nothing moves. But people have feelings, and those feelings matter. Good feelings support retention, build team cohesion, morale, and contribute to the workplace as a positive experience. Let's agree that feelings are important. Let's agree that it's important to feel important.

The managers in this situation were OBE. The extended meetings revealed a long-standing lack of communication. Once the communication began, it was nearly impossible to stifle, and revealed a host of concerns that were too numerous for the managers to address all at once. Many of the managers understood the root cause of the problem. Some of those who did said things such as "The meetings were taking a while, but we heard things we needed to hear, and that was valuable." The intent of the meeting was to place safety before the drivers each week, but the result gained much more than that.

What should you do when faced with a similar situation? The first lesson is to be aware that as a leader, you may be sought out for communication at any time. Whatever your subordinates expect from you, it begins with communication. Be alert for the signs that people project. Some will be very open, and approach you with their concerns. Others may not be as confident, and need to feel reassured that you will be available and interested. Most important, they need to feel that you will deliver.

The second item of importance is to determine which of the concerns you can address at your level, and which must be escalated to higher management. You will be perceived as a leader by your own subordinates as you address their concerns. You will also be perceived as a leader by upper management when you bring those concerns to their attention and have a plan to resolve them. Often, addressing a local issue that is unknown or ignored by other colleagues solves a problem for the entire organization. Everyone wins.

Some of the managers approached the problem with a certain amount of creativity. The schedules of the drivers and managers were often at odds. The managers had day-to-day responsibilities in sales and administration, and communicated daily with corporate during normal working hours. The drivers kept very different schedules, and some went weeks before seeing their manager, relying on telephone and email to keep in touch. One answer to this difference in time is to appoint a senior or lead driver, who will act as a leader and point of contact with the manager. This can work, but you have to exercise care in whom you appoint, especially if there is a problem such as we saw in this case. The rest of the drivers must have confidence in the person you select. If not, the person can be perceived negatively, or as an attempt by you to deflect the problem by placing a buffer between you and the drivers. No matter whom you choose the goals and objectives of the position need to be clearly spelled out. One manager who faced the "long meeting" problem told me that it would be some time before she gave up the role of presiding over the meetings herself.

"It's important that I do it", she said. "I want them to know that it is important enough for me to devote whatever time is necessary to deliver the safety topic and hear them out on other concerns." That's leadership. It's not always dramatic or earth shaking, but often it takes the shape of seemingly unimportant activities that are not revealed except by their absence.

One of the positive outcomes of the addition of structure to a management system is that it defines a time for certain events to take place. People can prepare in advance because they know what to expect. In the case of the long meeting, we discovered problems and concerns that went above the level of the area managers that needed to be addressed by corporate. Once we worked through the backlog of long standing issues, the meetings became closer in time to the ideal of ten minutes, and focused on safety alone. In a perfect world, the ten-minute meeting would have been in place and issues would have been addressed as they came up. But the company had grown by acquisition, and the safety meeting structure had not been part of the growth process. While we are praising the merits of structure, let's be practical. Once you put a structure in place, don't expect communication to blossom without some work. You need to monitor and assure the quality of communication and participation by the group members. You can rely on it too much, and the effect is the same as if you had no structure at all.

A CIRCUIT DESIGN PROBLEM?

"The most important thing in communication is hearing what isn't said."

Peter Drucker

CASE OBJECTIVES

- ○ To reveal the use of teaching moments by a leader
- ○ To differentiate between technical competency and leadership and why leaders must know the difference

CONTEXT

One of the leaders of a major electronics manufacturer assembled a team of engineers to design a particularly challenging circuit. The team leader he appointed was a very bright engineer, but he lacked skill in leading people, and the leader intended to make this a learning process for the engineer. He felt that the engineer would likely try to find the solution to the design by himself and would not fully utilize the skills of the team. After a period of time had passed, the team leader was called in to report on the team progress. The team leader showed the progress by sketching the completed parts of the circuit on a white board, and then remarked that *he* was at an impasse as to what the remainder of the circuit looked like.

- ○ **What questions should the leader ask of the engineer?**

In a brilliant and surprising move, the leader sketched the remainder of the circuit on the whiteboard, and just as quickly, erased it.

- ○ **Discuss the rationale of the leader. Why did he use this brief but very illustrative process to explain his motives to the team leader?**

This is another example of showing and not telling. Leaders do not always have the time to use a long and slow process to illustrate their concepts. This man was a brilliant leader whose name was well known in the American business community. At the time this event occurred, he was managing a company of over one hundred thousand people worldwide. But he was a very effective user of his own time.

- ○ **Discuss the effect of the event on the team leader.**

If you are the leader of nine other people, and you tend you disregard their input, you have lost 90% of the team's collective intelligence. Leaders get things done through and with people.

LATE NIGHT CALLS

> "Success is not final, failure is not fatal: it is the courage to continue that counts."
>
> **Winston Churchill**

CASE OBJECTIVES

- ○ To develop a sense of the need for analysis in the new leader
- ○ To pursue the development of confidence in followers
- ○ To assess the status of training in followers

CONTEXT

A manager takes over leadership of a group of truck drivers who operate on a 24/7 basis. He is given a Blackberry with which to communicate with his drivers. There are no shift supervisors, and each of the 20 drivers reports to the manager directly. For the first several weeks, his Blackberry is very active and he receives calls around the clock. Few if any of the calls are necessary, but the drivers seem tentative and not inclined to make decisions on their own.

- ○ **In forming a leadership plan, what issues does a new leader need to pursue?**
- ○ **As a new leader, it is often necessary to assess the culture of the group within the larger organization. Discuss the apparent culture of this group.**

The new manager is trying to make a determination about what is happening. He considers that the drivers may be testing him to determine how much freedom they have in making decisions on their own, but he also considers what the previous manager may have been like.

- ○ **What do you believe is happening?**
- ○ **Why do you think it is happening?**

- **Do you need more information to determine what is occurring?**

The new manager determines that the previous manager was extremely control oriented. The drivers lacked confidence and referred every possible issue to him, regardless of how small.

- **Discuss what type of leadership may be necessary to resolve the issues among the drivers. What actions might the new manager take to change the culture?**

After a few more nights of numerous telephone calls, he begins to ask each driver of his opinion regarding the situation, and to ask the driver what he thinks he should do in each case. He is gratified by the answers he receives, and determines that the drivers have been trained well and display good judgment, but have never been trusted to make decisions on their own.

At the next meeting of the group, he tells the drivers that they need not call him except in cases of accidents or property damage. He tells them that they will possibly make a few mistakes in their judgment calls, but that most of the mistakes will not place the company in jeopardy or place their jobs at risk. He lets them know that he has enough trust in them to do this. The calls decreased as the drivers began to understand that they now had a leader who believed in them.

In a tightly controlled and transactional environment there is room for only one authority. There is little use for judgment at an individual level under these conditions. Trust is a quality which develops individual sharpness and responsibility.

How many managers or leaders do you know who will accept the culture as it is and continue without making the changes necessary? Change is a primary role of real leaders.

MARCH TO THE SOUND OF THE CANNONS

"Where will I be found? March to the sound of the guns. That is where you will find me."

Napoleon

CASE OBJECTIVES

- ○ To instill in new leaders the need for presence in crisis
- ○ To understand the dynamics of failing to be present and its consequences
- ○ To enable the new leader to distinguish between doing things right and doing the right thing

CONTEXT

You are the CEO of a small company. It is late Thursday, and you have just learned that one of your people has had an accident in a company vehicle and killed someone at an intersection. While the company has had employee deaths, this is the first time someone outside of the company has been killed. It seems that the evidence shows the company driver to have been at fault. The accident occurred at a city in the Northeast, and it would take several hours to get there by plane. The local manager has never had to deal with the press, and the driver who was responsible for the accident is very upset. The accident is featured on the local news. The regional manager responsible for the area is on vacation but calls in for information. A meeting is held to determine next steps. You give the local manager your cell and home telephone numbers and state that you are available should anyone need you. The meeting is convened. The safety manager asks you if you would consider going to the area to assist. You respond that if they need you, they can call, and then ask him what exactly what would you do even if you were there. The safety manager, who has no line responsibility for the staff at the accident site, then makes arrangements for himself and travels to the area to assist the local staff with several issues.

- ○ **Who becomes the de facto leader in this event?**
- ○ **What is the effect of the CEO's absence on the field, especially at the site involved in the accident?**
- ○ **What might be some reasons for the CEO to avoid being present at the site?**
- ○ **Should the CEO and Region Manager have gone to the site? Why? Why not?**
- ○ **Discuss the difference between doing things right and doing the right thing? Which of these occurred in this case?**
- ○ **The case was a very big media event. Could this fact have caused the CEO to remain away from the scene?**

In a pure transactional sense, the CEO could have considered certain issues. He would review the company liability in such an accident and conclude that the mechanism is in place to deal with the financial results of the accident. His comments after the accident seemed to indicate that there was nothing he felt he could offer other than to be present, as was revealed to the various corporate staff immediately after the event. These all would have met the appropriate standard for "doing things right".

True leaders desire to be where the action is occurring. In Army terms, they ". . . march to the sounds of the cannons". They understand that their presence can act as support for their followers in difficult times, and they want to be involved in these types of challenges. By failing to appear, the regional manager and CEO relinquished the role of leaders. They left their people without support in a time when leadership was needed. Once that type of absence has been noted by the field, the only thing remaining for them is the title. The people in the field get the message that when the chips fall and things get tough, their "leaders" will not share the difficulties with them.

In this case, the Operations Group became the focus of the field as they answered questions, supported the affected location by phone and physical presence. They became the de facto leaders in this event because of the absence of the CEO and Regional Manager.

THE NEW OPERATING ROOM NURSE

"Thaw with her gentle persuasion is more powerful than Thor with his hammer. The one melts, the other breaks into pieces."

Henry David Thoreau

CASE OBJECTIVES

○ Demonstrate the need for persuasion no matter what the position
○ Shows the need for buy-in among a group so that critical decisions are arrived at with full support

CONTEXT

During the 1950's in the Deep South, race was still an issue, and most all facilities were segregated between blacks and whites. A Hospital Administrator, in a casual conversation with one of his black nurse's aides, learned that her son would be getting out of the Army after serving for several years as a Medical Corpsman and later an operating room nurse-technician at the Army's prestigious Walter Reed Hospital. The administrator asked her what his plans were once he came home, and she replied that he would probably get a job as a laborer or truck driver.

He asked that she provide him with her son's resume. She did, and the administrator found that the young man had not only experienced combat as a medic in Korea, but had been extensively trained in operating room procedures. He felt that the young man would be a great asset for the staff and would be able to assist the doctors in many of their surgical procedures. The administrator has the authority to hire the young man on his own.

- What risk does the Administrator assume if he hires the man on his own, without consulting the physicians for their thoughts?
- How might you bring the young man into your organization without causing issues among the staff and patients?
- Consider whether in this situation you would be interested in hiring the young man.
- What is in the best interests of the organization?
- Of the community?

Aware of the possibility of resistance to a black man in the operating room, he decided to present the resume without a name to see if the physicians felt as he did regarding the soldier's qualifications. He made copies of the resume and distributed them to the staff physicians, and over a period of time asked their opinion. Only when all of them had come to him with positive comments did he tell them who the young man was. To a man, they voiced their support in hiring. The fact that his mother was a known and competent staff member was helpful, but the use of persuasion by the administrator was certainly a factor. And the physicians themselves showed integrity in their acceptance of the man. The best leaders persuade, and do not order. Acting in this manner makes the process of acceptance a group effort. The staff doctors had fully agreed to the process of bringing the young soldier aboard, and they in turn would see to it that their patients would be told of his qualifications and their confidence in him. This narrative gives us two examples of leadership. The first is persuasion, but the second is influence. The physicians held the influence among their patients, and their agreement to the hiring of the former soldier assured a smooth transition for his entry into the organization.

SALES QUOTAS IN A MANUFACTURING COMPANY

"Eliminate numerical quotas, including Management
by Objectives."

W. Edwards Deming

CASE OBJECTIVES

- To understand that groups within a company may not possess compatible and supporting objectives.
- To enable the new leader to understand the need for various groups to align themselves with common objectives

CONTEXT

The CEO of a specialized manufacturer of electronic instruments was conducting a meeting with his regional sales managers when the subject of the next year's quotas entered the discussion. The quotas had already been promulgated, and the CEO casually asked the managers how they thought they would perform against the quotas. Each of the sales managers eagerly stated their expectations, and most of the sales staff were emphatic that they would exceed the quotas in the coming cycle.

The CEO then informs them that he wants to discuss with them some of the *negative* consequences of *exceeding* their quotas.

- **What should the relationship/interaction be between sales and production in a manufacturing environment?**
- **What is the effect of unexpected large orders in such an operation?**

The CEO then began a discussion about the "why" of quotas and how they should be used. He reminded them that as a manufacturing company, the internal operations such as procurement and assembly required predictable and orderly amounts of components flowing into the system. Large and unexpected orders often were more costly, since they might require expedited shipments from suppliers for which the company paid a higher price. He went on to say that once quotas were established, he needed the sales force to try to meet them, and told them that a 5% plus or minus the stated quota was the most efficient way to plan production. The sales managers had never heard anything like this before. They had always been programmed to break quotas, the higher the better. Now they had a CEO who was telling them that he needed them to understand the manufacturing process, and how their efforts were needed to assist that process. He was bringing them into the heart of the company in a way that no one had.

A major lesson is to be found in this example. The sales managers were in the field with customers and sales representatives daily. They attended management meetings at company headquarters infrequently, and always chafed at being away from the action. In this type of situation it is not unusual for an adversarial relationship to develop. Salesmen may become irritated when the shipment for a prized customer is late, or when the answer to a technical question is not quickly forthcoming. Often they see themselves as the only people who care about the customer. They reason that they are responsible for what drives the profit engine and that if 100% of quota is good, and then 110% surely is better.

As a leader, the CEO recognized the need to align the requirements of his manufacturing group with the performance of the sales force. Leaders must understand what motivates their followers with respect to the organizational objectives. The level of alignment is different for certain groups. Both the CEO and managers understood that from time to time there would be variances in the quotas. Large orders would sometimes occur well in excess of quotas, but the sales force now understood that if those events seemed likely, they should give advance notice to production so that orders could be met on time without incurring excessive procurement costs. Leaders have to determine just how much information is too much, and how much is absolutely necessary.

THE 7 AM SUPPORT CALL

"Email, instant messaging, and cell phones give us fabulous communication ability, but because we live and work in our own little worlds, that communication is totally disorganized."

Marilyn vos Savant

CASE OBJECTIVES

- ○ For new leaders to understand the nature of support and their obligations in delivering it

CONTEXT

A Project Manager in a large IT consulting company was involved in a project away from the home office and experienced several technical problems. There were several teams in the field across the United States, and he worked directly for the overall executive in charge of the roll-out. The project was technical, involving electrical and mechanical equipment and software, and required several days at each of the sites before completion.

The executive in charge of roll-out conducted a 7 A.M. meeting via conference call with each of his team leaders. During that call, each gave a verbal status report for the preceding day's activities, and then discussed what our problems and needs were for the next day's work. There were many occasions in such a technical project when each team leader had exceeded his knowledge and required help. The large corporate structure of EDS possessed a huge pool of talent. On one such morning the Project Manager had determined that he needed an electrical engineer and a software analyst. Often the needs were immediate, as in order to affect a fix, it became necessary to cease production at the client facility.

This is unprofitable, and has to be done quickly. He told the client executive of the needs he had, and he responded. "Call me back by 9 AM; I will have them on a conference call for you."

- **What leadership quality does the client executive display in this instance?**

Army Officers and NCO's would use the term "carrying water for their troops" to describe this event. The client executive understood that the Project Manager was extremely busy with the events happening at the scene. To try to navigate the company hierarchy under those circumstances would have been nearly impossible and it would have taken a long time. He realized that he was the proper resource and acted accordingly. He was a leader. A manager would probably not have done this.

- **What is the effect on the morale and confidence of the Project Manager when working with such a client executive?**
- **What are the effects on the *transactional* portion of the project?**
- **Discuss the synergy of transactional and transformational in this case.**
- **What will the reaction of the client be in this case?**

This kind of supportive response is great for the morale of the leader in the field. Faced with the unpleasant task of informing the client that he needs to stop production for a time, you can get very uncomfortable. But when you know that someone at corporate is carrying water for you, making your job easier, your confidence increases dramatically, and some of the pressure is reduced. You feel confident that the solution to any problem is in your organization, and your leader is going to find someone who will deliver the resource to you. When the means to achieve is clearly available, the confidence of the leader will grow remarkably. This case also exhibits the use of structure and communication done according to a schedule. It provides predictable support that is very important to a field leader who faces difficult problems each day, and its 24-hour cycle time allows for a fairly rapid response to questions needed for support.

WORKING BOY AND MR. JOHN SLEDGE

"Faced with what is right, to leave it undone shows a lack of courage."

Confucius

CASE OBJECTIVES

- ○ Leaders should understand the Ethic of Reciprocity
- ○ Leaders need to know that leadership is sometimes simple kindness
- ○ Entering the organization is an important process which should be attended to with care
- ○ True leadership can occur at any level in the organization

CONTEXT

During my first college summer I worked construction in South Louisiana. I reported for work the first day and was acquainted with my equipment, a single sixteen-pound sledge. The company was remodeling an old school, and my first task was to take down an interior wall. There were three of us on the sledge that first day. My companions were two black men, Working Boy and Roman. Both had been working construction most of their lives, were well muscled and conditioned. I went at the wall with a vengeance. At lunch, I sat down to eat, and my hands had already turned bloody and stiff. Working Boy leaned over across his sandwich and said "Lemme me see them hands, Slim." He took both of my hands in his and shook his head. "Cain't work with them hands, Slim. End of the day, Mr. John Sledge be standin' tall, you'll be a broke man. After lunch, we gonna show you how to work Mr. Sledge". Lunch over, Working Boy beckoned with a muscular arm and I followed. In a series of brief instructions, he told me how to handle the sledge. "Ease up on the sledge, Slim. Work it slow but steady. Swing the sledge and let it do the work. Pay attention to your grip on the handle." He showed me his technique, and then made me show him mine. He told me how to select a pair of gloves that would be best for the kind of work we were facing over the next few months, and then he told me how to treat my hands when I went home after work. The lesson lasted fifteen minutes. Forty plus years later, I remember his name, his face, and his voice. Leadership takes many forms. He could have shrugged me off, a white college kid who was only going to work construction until college was done, but he didn't. He looked around at the job, saw me as one of the resources, took action to coach me and in doing so, displayed true leadership. I came to work the next day with bandaged hands, proper gloves, and a good sledge form. Mr. Sledge and I became, if not great friends, proper acquaintances. There is one unknown in the story, and that is the leadership skills of the company manager. I can guess that he was probably pretty good with people, and that Working Boy had been encouraged to coach me by his own positive experiences. This is an example of managing the entry. It can be simple, as this was, or complex in a factory environment where safety is a critical issue.

- **Discuss the action of Working Boy. Was he displaying leadership or simple kindness? Is there a difference?**
- **Does this event tell us anything about whether leadership can occur even at the lowest levels of an organization?**
- **Does your organization assign mentors or "helpmates" for new employees?**

There are tangible and intangible effects produced by leadership. In my case, I was able to work the next day without pain and to accomplish my job effectively. I had a bit more confidence because of Working Boy. I knew that if I had a question or problem I could approach him. The transactional and the transformational were equally attended by his action towards me. Training is important, and sometimes it generates a benefit beyond proficiency in the specific task. An example of this occurs when trainees develop a sense of belonging and mission over and above the details of the task for which they are being trained. We look at the actions of someone like Working Boy as kindness, but it is important to note that they are also elements of leadership.

We tend in this society to link leadership with the famous, but that isn't necessarily accurate. We also think of leadership as the province of the focal leader, the person appointed by the organization with the title and the task of directing the fortunes of the company. The more complete truth is that the appointed leader can only lead with the support and cooperation of everyone in the organization. And everyone in the organization can lead, in many ways. The story of Working Boy is a good example of the paradigm of leadership at all levels. What would be the effect on an organization populated by dozens of people like Working Boy?

We need to be reminded that humans populate organizations. What a concept! It is still remarkable to me that despite the simplicity of this concept, we have to reinforce it continually. When we accept that, we deliver a message of humanity to the workplace that affects everyone in it. Why is it that decades after I spent time getting acquainted with Mr. Sledge, I still remember Working Boy? It's because the small kindness he showed toward me touched my humanity. These kinds of lessons tend to be remembered far longer than anything found in an MBA classroom or business course.

THE TEN AND TWENTY-FIVE PERCENT SOLUTION

> "The leader has to be practical and a realist, yet must talk the language of the visionary and the idealist."
>
> **Eric Hoffer**

CASE OBJECTIVES

- To provide an example of shared sacrifice and its use as a motivator for leaders

CONTEXT

A small specialized company which provides data services to the U.S. government depends on contract approvals on a timely basis to maintain their level of staff. At some point, the contract is delayed and the company faces layoffs of valued personnel. The company is certain that the contract will be awarded but it may take some time. During that time, cash will be short.

Assume that you are the CEO. What options do you have? You know the contract will be renewed, but also know that you will have a cash flow problem which will exist for perhaps three months or more. You have selected your staff carefully and wish to retain as many of them as possible.

The company leadership took aggressive measures to minimize staff losses. They announced that they would take salary reductions of 25% and asked for voluntary employee reductions of 10%. Over time, as the contract was closer to renewal, they brought some employees back to work and retained others, then brought the pay back to the former levels.

Downward loyalty of this kind is rare in corporations. The trend is usually moving in the other direction, to greater compensation and less risk for leadership and less compensation and more risk for employees.

    o **Discuss your emotional reaction to this event. Assume you are an employee who took the 10% reduction and now are back on regular pay.**

THE CUSTOMER IS NOT ALWAYS RIGHT

> "The very essence of leadership is its purpose. And the purpose of leadership is to accomplish a task. That is what leadership does—and what it does is more important than what it is or how it works."
>
> **Colonel Dandridge M. Malone**

CASE OBJECTIVES

- To demonstrate the effect of policy designed around external factors on morale

CONTEXT

This case occurred in a retail electronics environment. The company in which it occurred is no longer operating.

A customer brought in a box containing a low-cost video camera, complaining that the box indicated that the camera was a high-end model but when he opened it he discovered the cheaper model. He wanted a store credit which would be the price of the high-end camera. The sales person checked the computer for past purchases by this customer, and discovered that the customer had in fact bought two video cameras, one at the high price and another of lesser cost at different stores of the company. He quickly understood what was happening, and refused the credit. Over the next few weeks, the drama continued to play out as the customer gradually worked the challenge up the hierarchy while being refused at every level. Finally, several weeks later, a regional Vice-President received and honored the customer's request for a refund over the objections of the local and district personnel. He does this without issuing a clarification of the policy for future guidance.

○ **What potential problems do you see as a result of the actions of the regional Vice-President?**

The Vice-President has now essentially guaranteed that any such further issues will be escalated to him for resolution. This will also cause a loss of morale among the sales staff. Rather than being complimented for their action in protecting the company's bottom line, they are likely to become demoralized and confused, and will believe that the company does not care about their efforts. There will also be a problem with the lack of consistency in the manner of how these types of issues should be handled. The VP believed that he solved the problem with the customer, but in doing so he created a problem for leadership throughout the organization.

FORCED RANKING

> "I used to think that running an organization was equivalent to conducting a symphony orchestra. But I don't think that's quite it; it's more like jazz. There is more improvisation."
>
> **Warren Bennis**

CASE OBJECTIVES

- To generate discussion on an important human relations issue
- To reveal the effects of a policy designed to "trade up" among personnel

CONTEXT

During the time that Jack Welch was CEO of General Electric, he instituted a ranking mandate. Each personnel rating period, supervisors were instructed that they must assign the lowest ranking to 10% of all personnel they rated. In current terminology, this is called "forced ranking".

- **Do you believe that the evaluation of personnel as a mandated "quota" is appropriate for a leader? Discuss.**
- **Is the 10% solution a fair practice?**
- **What effect does the 10% mandate have on a leader's skill in development of the bottom 10%? i.e., does the leader develop skill in attending to the needs of the 10% or does he simply neglect them?**
- **Many people will defend the 10% solution by reminding us that under Welch, GE was very productive. Discuss whether or not this is meaningful.**

This practice is controversial. Many will argue that it is part of the survival of the fittest in a competitive workplace. Others disagree. Regardless of the belief in its practicality, the process of forced ranking begs several questions. In the military, officer fitness reports and enlisted evaluations provide for ranking, but in the middle and lower ranks, forced ranking is not typically used. There has recently been a form of forced ranking that seeks to limit the inflation of evaluation rankings, but this affects primarily accelerated promotions. This occurs despite the fact that a military evaluation form is a highly structured and quantitatively oriented device. (Here the instructor/facilitator may use an appropriate form to demonstrate)

One of the challenges to a forced ranking system is when/if there is a lack of objective standards and criteria. If forced ranking is to be used, great care should be taken that goals and objectives are clear, and that the person evaluated has been given adequate support to achieve them. This support includes the active participation of the evaluating leader.

- **As of 2003, more than 30% of all U.S. corporations queried used or planned to use the forced ranking system. Does this imply that there is an implicit understanding that 10% of the hires are flawed by design?**
- **Does the type of organizational structure and personnel imply a more eager attempt to adopt a forced ranking system? For example, is a highly technical company populated by scientists and engineers more likely to use such a system? How about the military?**

EXPENSE REPORT ISSUES

"Education without values, as useful as it is, seems rather to make man a more clever devil."

C.S. Lewis

CASE OBJECTIVES

○ To point out the importance of clarity in procedures and how its lack can sometimes cause challenges for leaders

CONTEXT

You are the team leader for a group of technicians working in various cities. The team stays in hotels, and is given a $35.00 per day meal allowance. In the particular city where most of the work is done, the average daily expenditure is significantly less than the $35.00 allowance. As team leader, you rarely exceed the meal allowance. However, one of the team consistently declares expenses exactly for the full amount each day.

○ **Given the difference between the other reports of expenses being below the $35.00 daily allowance, what is your response as a leader toward the team member claiming the full amount daily?**
○ **Do you have the correct information to make a decision on the action of the team member?**

The company had not defined the meal allowance adequately for the team leaders in this instance. He checked with accounting and learned that accounting considered the $35.00 as a per diem. Does this new information change your opinion of the team member who declares the full amount each day? Assume that the overage per day is $10.00 or $50.00/week x 50 weeks = $2,500.

○ **As a leader, do you change your opinion of the team member who takes the full amount each day**?

You probably should not bias your opinion of the team member negatively. You are entitled to some congratulation from the company for looking out for their money as if it were your own. If the amount is defined as per diem, the company will charge that amount back to the client. It is expedient, and costs less in the long run because analyzing each report for a large company would cost a significant amount of money. It is a matter of expediency.

SAFETY BONUS?

> "Motivation is simple. You eliminate those who are not motivated."
>
> **Lou Holtz**

CASE OBJECTIVES

- Demonstrate the need to understand the difference between the achievement of a simple quota when a true behavioral change is needed

CONTEXT

A company hires a safety manager to review their operations and propose methods to reduce accidents and incidents. As a part of the new methods, the company agrees to establish safety bonuses for managers who complete one year without any accidents or incidents. The safety manager also travels throughout the various locations, and audits safety processes and procedures, asking safety oriented questions of employees and estimating compliance with the new standards. He visits one particular location and observes that the manager is unfamiliar with the standards and his employees do not seem to be interested. He further observes several safety violations. At year end, the location in question is nominated for a safety award as they have fulfilled the accident free requirement despite their disinterested attitude toward safety.

- **You are the Safety Manager, what should you do in this case?**

The Safety Manager recommends to the CEO and HR Manager that the manager be denied the bonus due to a lack of compliance with safety directives.

You are the CEO. What should you do?

The CEO is concerned that morale will suffer if the bonus is not granted, and denies the Safety Managers recommendation. He's also concerned about fairness. He grants the bonus.

- **What do you think the net effect of the granting of the safety award will be on the other managers who have complied with the safety requirements yet had minor accidents?**

Leadership above all is about change, and almost always about changing the habits of people toward a more productive, and in this case, safe work environment. Luck should not enter in to the calculation for bonuses and awards if behavior is not being modified. That is one takeaway from this event. Another is that if you are going to propose bonuses and awards, the criteria must be carefully defined. While the end result was met in this case, the enabling factors of changed behavior were not present. As a result, other managers who had worked hard to effect safety changes were not rewarded for their efforts, which resulted in a loss of morale and a feeling that they were unfairly treated.

MONEY BALL-CONSTRAINTS AND CREATIVITY

"Anxiety is the hand maiden of creativity."

T. S. Eliot

CASE OBJECTIVES
(May be done as a major case by having participants read the book or selected portions of the book, or watch the movie)

- Reveal the challenges in changing long standing traditions and beliefs held in an organization
- To examine the necessity of searching for the truth, not the assumptions that pass for truth in organizations
- To demonstrate how the necessity of constraint may bring about creative solutions

CONTEXT

Billy Beane was a remarkably talented high school athlete. By his senior year in a California high school, Beane was being sought by various colleges, and had been offered a scholarship to Stanford where he expected to play football and baseball. Beane mulled over the situation with his parents, and instead of Stanford, accepted an offer to play major league baseball.

Beane had a lackluster career among the pros, and never developed into the player that scouts were certain he would become. After his playing career ended, he found a position with the Oakland Athletics and eventually became their general manager. In the Oakland job, Beane was forced to deal with a severely limited budget compared with other major league baseball teams. From the beginning of his management career, Beane had ideas that diverged from the baseball traditionalists. With his fresh ideas he was controversial, especially among scouts and long time baseball staffers. One of his first encounters with tradition came when he hired a Yale educated graduate in Economics to exhaustively analyze baseball statistics. This was the beginning of a new era in baseball scouting and drafting. Beane aggressively challenged the opinions of the Oakland scouting staff, relying instead on hard statistics before drafting players. In the case of high school pitchers for example, he urged scouts to remember that high school pitchers had "young" arms, untested and unchallenged over the short seasons in high schools. He preferred pitchers with more seasoned arms, such as college players. He looked even harder at batting averages, preferring instead to look at things such as on-base percentages. That, he said, indicated more about a players potential value than other statistics. Beane enjoyed great success as a General Manager, and was offered a huge sum to leave Oakland for the Boston Red Sox to implement his methods in their organization, but refused. His rationale was that the only time he had ever done anything for money was his signing bonus and subsequent failure to attend Stanford.

- Which valuable characteristics as a leader did Beane exhibit in his approach?
- Discuss the difficulty of changing long-standing established cultures
- What methods may be used to change such cultures?
- What did the role of a constrained supply of money to acquire players have in the development of Beane's strategies?
- Why did Beane see the changes needed when no one else did?

Beane challenged the conventional wisdom of the truth. He refused to accept the traditional version of the truth because he had experienced it as a young athlete. It is very important for every new leader to reassess the version of the truth as presented to him. Assess the facts presented to you and evaluate them on your own.

THE HOSPITAL EMERGENCY PLAN

> "Let our advance worrying become advance thinking and planning."
>
> **Winston Churchill**

CASE OBJECTIVES

- ○ Examine the need for vision and asking "what if" in a service organization
- ○ Demonstrate how vision and planning will work without its creator if well done

CONTEXT

In the early 1960's, a hospital administrator takes charge of a hospital of 200 beds situated on the Gulf Coast of Louisiana. One of his first acts upon arriving was to assess the ability of the hospital to respond to an emergency on a large scale, such as an industrial accident or fire. He learned that there was no such plan in effect and immediately began the process of developing the plan with the staff. It was before cell phones were available, and the administrator and his family were occupying a newly rented house and the phone company had not yet arrived to deliver service. As he arrived for work early one morning, he noticed the presence of many police cars and a helicopter landing on the hospital parking lot. Something serious had happened. An oil drilling ship had caught fire offshore, with numerous killed and injured, and the casualties were being brought to the hospital.

As he entered the hospital he witnessed people going about their duties with calm and purpose. The plan that had been worked out with the staff was in place, and there seemed to be little for him to do. At that point he simply made the rounds of each of the staff positions designated by the plan to see if there was anything he needed to do for his staff, and noted a few problems with the plan and marked them for future changes.

- **Leaders ask "what if" continually. How does this process of questioning contribute to long term vision for leaders?**
- **The role of planning is typically considered one of the typical transactional objectives of managers. How does this event differ from the traditional role of planning? Does it move toward the transformational?**
- **What is the worst event possible for this organization? Have you defined it? Are you ready for it?**
- **Who are the potential leaders in your group on which you can depend to respond to the "worst event"?**

The primary lesson in this case is of the need for vision. Leaders must ask the question "what if . . . ?." What if an employee does not appear for work? What will we do if we have a computer failure? What is our response to accidents? I once attended a safety meeting where a manager told me that he was not going to put a safety regulation in place "just because there might be an accident". The possible and probable can become reality quickly. If we are not prepared for them, we will probably fail. The administrator had the vision that the scope of his responsibilities were broad and that they encompassed a possible disaster to which he and his staff would have to respond. You cannot wish away possible problems or deny their existence. Within reason, you must have the vision and foresight to plan a response. The second issue in this example is that you cannot delegate broad responsibility. The vision to accept the necessity of preparing an emergency action plan was the responsibility of the administrator. The authority to carry out individual segments of the plan was delegated. Once a good plan is in place, leaders watch but rarely micromanage. They trust their appointed on-scene leadership to make adjustments and corrections as needed, and this trust becomes part of a learning and risk taking culture that supports the organization during challenging events. Planning asks the question "what if" and answers the question "if, then".

PENN STATE AND PATERNO

"More often there's a compromise between ethics and expediency."

Peter Singer

CASE OBJECTIVES

- ○ To reveal the consequences of failing to fully address the issues of a case involving personnel misconduct of a serious nature
- ○ To distinguish the differences between doing things right and doing the right thing

CONTEXT

In July of 2012, the former Director of the FBI, Louis Freeh, released the results of an eight month investigation into the sexual abuse of young children on the Penn State campus. Just weeks prior to the completion of the investigation, former Assistant Penn football coach Jerry Sandusky had been found guilty of more than forty cases of such abuse. The investigation was conducted to determine the extent of the crimes and to determine just how many people had been aware of the abuse, and the results were shocking. As early as 1998, a graduate assistant coach had reported to the head coach Joe Paterno, that he had seen Sandusky engaging in sexual acts with a young man who was a participant in a program called "The Second Mile", which was run by Sandusky and founded to assist young men at risk. The investigation revealed that among those who were aware of the abuse included the President of the University, the Athletic Director, the Vice President for Business and Finance, the Attorney General, and Paterno. It had been nearly fifteen years since the initial allegations were reported, and it is likely that scores of people became aware of the events over that time period. In addition to the involvement at the highest levels, janitors who worked in the building where the assaults occurred were fearful of reporting the abuse because they could have lost their jobs. Paterno and football were king, and the culture was corrupt from the top down. Sandusky will likely spend the remainder of his life in prison, but what of the culpability of the others?

- ○ **Can you account for the failure of anyone in the organization to protect the children from abuse?**
- ○ **Is this problem primarily moral and ethical or are there other factors involved in the lack of leadership?**
- ○ **What actions would you have taken in the very first instance of learning about the abuse in 1998?**
- ○ **What if you were told that it was not what it seemed, or to stay out of it because it had been reported and was being resolved, yet you saw it happen again? How far would you go?**

This is an example of a long standing and well entrenched culture that protects its members. It was learned that the Attorney General of the State at the time of the abuses later became the Governor. There are times when cultures can only be changed through their complete leveling. This would appear to have been one of those. The tragedy is that it took so long to achieve. In this case the protection of the reputation of the institution was deemed so necessary that crimes were permitted against individuals, not once, but over a period of years. The people in the chain of command in the University placed their obligations to the University above their obligations to the young men who were abused.

- ○ **Place yourself in the position of the first person known to have become aware of the abuse, the Assistant Coach. Could he have done anything differently?**

We do not have all of the facts regarding the abuse without reading the FBI report. We can however make some assumptions. We can assume that the graduate assistant felt comfortable in going to Paterno, who he felt was a man of some character. He may have been told that the issue was under investigation, and on that basis felt that he had done the right thing. Laws have letters, and laws have spirit. Moral ethics requires that we follow both.

THOUGHT LEADERSHIP AND VISION

"Every man takes the limits of his own field of vision for the limits of the world."

Arthur Schopenhauer

CASE OBJECTIVES

- To enable a new leader to distinguish between practical and impractical vision
- To present the seductive vision of new technology along with its challenges

CONTEXT

A young business analyst begins working for a small consulting group. In one of his first assignments, the director discusses a problem he is having with the chairman and directors of a mid-sized construction company with a good reputation in building chemical plants and refineries. The time frame is the early 1980's, and new technology is everywhere. The director is insistent that he wants to take the company into a new and fast paced arena. The consulting group director is just as certain that the construction company does not belong in such a fast paced environment and assigns the young analyst the task of giving a presentation to the board of directors that will change their minds.

- **How might you dissuade the chairman from his high technology vision?**

The analyst crafts a presentation that illustrates the history of four devices, beginning with the weight scale, then the clock, the internal combustion engine, and finally the semiconductor. He shows the gradually faster progression in the utility and capability of each device, ending with the remarkably rapid and continuing updating of the semiconductor. He then posed the challenge of responding to such a market with the current company business model, and how the company would have to internally change in a dramatic and significant manner to compete in such an environment. The consulting group had already developed an alternative model more suited to the company's capabilities, but until the difficulties were shown, they had little success in moving the group away from the high technology into a more suitable environment.

While vision is necessary to move forward, it is sometimes seduced by an impractical external environment and a lack of internal resources sufficient to meet the vision.

THE SIX WEEK ITINERARY

> "The single biggest problem with communication is the illusion that it has taken place."
>
> **George Bernard Shaw**

CASE OBJECTIVES

○ How a measure designed to actively support non-direct reports can be utilized

CONTEXT

This case took place in the early 1970's, before cell phones and laptops were available. The marketing manager of a major chemical company which makes specialty chemicals and radioactive tracers for research does not have direct responsibility for the sales force, but still needs to be able to reach out in a timely manner and provide marketing information to them which is critical to the sales process. He institutes a process whereby each of the sales people must provide him with a continually updated six-week itinerary. The itinerary required not only customer names to be visited, but also a contact number at a hotel or motel. Some of the people in the sales force resist this measure.

○ **Why in your opinion do the sales people resist this effort?**

The sales force was not made aware of the Market Manager's purpose of the new requirement. The manager of the sales force had not had time to discuss the measure with the Market Manager. They also resisted a requirement from someone not in their chain of command. The purpose of the new measure was to provide the Market Manager with an idea of what types of institutions the sales force would be in contact with over the coming six week period. He intended to use it to support the field sales force. As the Market

Manager, he was aware of developments in the company that happened very quickly and needed to know which markets would be well served by the new product development. He also wanted to use the sales force as a marketing tool. In many cases, he would telephone the hotel where the sales person was staying to inform them of a new product, and ask him to get information from the potential customer about the product and their opinion as well as the customer's technical requirements.

As leaders, we often must lead by influence and not through direct or institutional structure. In those cases, communication of our intent becomes critical. The Market Manager had a great system given the limits of communication in that era, but he needed to "persuade" more and "tell" less. Eventually the purpose of the measure was made known, and the sales force saw it as a great support tool for their efforts. Resistance to change never changes.

COMMUNICATION—FROM CORPORATE TO THE FIELD

"Much unhappiness has come into the world because of bewilderment and things left unsaid."

Fyodor Dostoyevsky

CASE OBJECTIVES

○ To reveal the need for established communication channels and the difficulty of obtaining information without them

CONTEXT

The Chairman of the Board of Directors of an engineering company based in Europe has heard rumors that his UK Based Director is a very heavy-handed and caustic manager who has been antagonizing potential customers in the US. The Chairman has never met the staffs of the various US offices and few even know his name. He schedules a trip to the US headquarters, ostensibly to learn more of what is happening and obtain information about the problem. He announces that he wants open and frank communication, and plans a lunch meeting with the US staff. You are a member of the US staff, and have experienced firsthand how the manager has antagonized prospective customers. How will you handle the meeting?

○ **Discuss the possible outcomes of this meeting. Would you feel comfortable discussing your experiences with the Chairman? If not, why not?**
○ **Would you feel more comfortable with a one-on-one meeting with the Chairman than in a group setting?**

This is a fairly frequent type of occurrence in the corporate world. It rarely reveals the information sought after. Leaders at higher levels of the corporation rely on their position and title, expecting that it will ensure that they receive information. Often, when they do not receive the information, they assume that the rumors have no basis.

Leaders who truly wish to know what is happening cannot simply fly in, have lunch with people they have never met, and expect open and honest communication. In other cases, we have seen how distance becomes a negative dimension for leaders. Presence and a long and unbroken line of communications open the channel so that information flows freely.

- ○ **How might the Chairman have ensured that his visit provided him with honest and open communication?**

Levels of organizational hierarchy act as upward filters. Leaders at high levels know this and act to establish channels outside of the hierarchy. The Chairman in question was not able to learn firsthand of the actions of his director. US staff did not know him well enough to talk freely, and did not know whether they could trust him. As we have seen in Case 8, "Skunks and Sycophants" one approach to this problem was used by General Hal Moore with his appointment of the unit skunk. The skunk is an informal position established by the leader early in the relationship, and his position is protected and endorsed by the leader. The military knows, from decades of experience, how to use "back channel" communication so that information flows upward freely. One example comes to mind from Desert Storm. General Norman Schwarzkopf leaves his aides behind and strides into a barracks. He sits down on a bunk next to a private and begins to ask questions. Later, a reporter asks him why he does this and intimates that he has staff to report on such things. Schwarzkopf replies that there are simply too many levels of hierarchy, and by the time information reaches him, it has been diluted. He goes further to comment that ". . . privates don't lie to Generals" or words to that effect.

Another avenue to using this form of communication would be to establish the practice of "Skip-level" evaluations. This is a practice that regularly evaluates leaders by going to the group for which the leader is responsible. By skipping the leader and going directly to his subordinates or followers, the evaluator can gain a sense of whether or not the leader is leading or simply transacting. In order for this to be successful and render fair and honest information, evaluators must be trained in the process.[34] It is also essential that the evaluator do these meetings on a consistent basis, and establish a trusting relationship for both the subordinate and the leader being evaluated.

GEORGE WASHINGTON—TRANSACTIONAL LEADER

To improve is to change; to be perfect is to change often.

Winston Churchill

CASE OBJECTIVES

- Establish the case for a structured and reasonable set of metrics in gauging group performance
- To show how the transactional application in an early life experience did not hinder later ability to act in a transformational manner
- To understand the place of a measurable transactional standard as a leadership tool

CONTEXT

In Richard Brookhiser's book, *George Washington on Leadership*, the author describes the hands on style practiced by Washington, from Washington's personal diary dated February 1760. From a day of checking progress on his plantation, Washington noted that four of his carpenters had spent one day in preparing 120 feet of trees into square-cut timber. Washington then engaged himself in what was an early time and motion study. "Sat down therefore and observed . . . Letting them proceed in their own way." Washington observed, oriented, decided, and then acted. (OODA loop)Based on his calculations he concluded that at the rate of production observed, each of the four men should be able to produce 125 feet of cut timber for every day of work. This is a quadrupling of the observed production. He then went further, and calculated that there would of necessity be differences in the rates of production for woods of varying density.

- ○ **Does the employment of such a transactional objective preclude the development of Washington as a transformational leader?**
- ○ **Of what value are the metrics developed by Washington?**

It is important that the transactional exist as a metric and benchmark. This does not exclude the practitioner of transactional management from becoming a transformational leader. In fact, employed properly, the transactional supports the intent of the transforming leader and enables them to grow.

- ○ **As a leader do you have reasonable metrics for your group?**
- ○ **Have you actively observed their work?**
- ○ **Do you understand the difficulties and challenges to the achievement of their stated performance indicators?**
- ○ **Have you provided the proper support environment, training, etc so that they can achieve these objectives? Ask that question *always*.**

WATER, MORE WATER!

"A fanatic is one who can't change his mind and won't change the subject."

Winston Churchill

CASE OBJECTIVES

- Reveal how a false sense of accomplishment can creep into a culture

CONTEXT

You are a consultant brought in to examine client performance against several objectives. Your specialty is in how processes and procedures benefit companies, and in this situation you are tasked with suggesting improvements to the processes and procedures used by the company. As you interview personnel during the engagement, you realize that the company has hired very capable people. You also find that the company resolves issues quickly. At first, this seems very positive and you are encouraged by what seem to be a series of quick resolutions of different pre-crisis events. In short, the company has been very good at "putting out fires". As you progress however, you begin to experience some concern for the manner in which the company operates.

- **What could be wrong with solving problems quickly?**
- **What concerns might the consultant have?**
- **What direction does the company culture seem to be leaning?**

As the consultant progresses in his work, he begins to see a pattern in how the company operates. He sees the same problem being addressed and solved multiple times.

- **What is happening here?**
- **How do you account for what is happening?**

The culture of this company has become one of hiring good people, and putting out fires, after which everyone is congratulated on the great job they did on avoiding catastrophe. People were congratulated and lauded for putting out fires, but when it came to finding the root causes of the problems and attacking them, the company lacked the element of accountability, and the discipline needed to do the difficult work of building a system that prevented fires and demanded responsibility for their cause. It is usually the case that solving a deep seated problem of any sort requires more time than addressing a quick fix, but equally true that the quick fix is rewarding and feels good *now*. Years later, after completing the project, the consultant had the opportunity to address the fire fighting culture with a colleague and friend who remained with the company. He said that the fire fighting culture was still in place, and accountability was still absent.

If we had to determine the most common attribute of organizational failures, we would be hard pressed to choose between communication and accountability. Both are required. But without accountability, failure is nearly a guarantee. While it is most commonly implemented in the rigid transactional organizational, it is absolutely critical to the success of the transformational leader. The transformational leader above all is interested in and dedicated to change above stability. To successfully promote change, we need to move away from comfort zones and account for that movement. Among military units, accountability is a dominant quality. It is a vital element of cohesive teams whether in sports or in business. The general premise is that accountability is demanded by superiors by subordinates. But to limit accountability to this narrow definition is to deny its importance and scope. Accountability is one of the building blocks of the leader who serves his people. They must know that he will support them, and he is accountable to them for support, motivation, and the creation of a positive environment. It is also important in building teams among peers, where its existence serves to build cohesiveness, because team members need to know that they are supported by peers when the situation demands it. The leader, in all instances, must ensure the presence and health of accountability.

In this event, changing the culture to addressing root causes was either uncomfortable or ignored by the company leadership. Everyone was comfortable with the ability of the firefighting team concept. Leaders go beyond their comfort zones and embrace change. In this case, in addition to the concept of accountability, it was necessary that the company see the change in accountability as a change in direction, away from the fighting of fires and toward the problems causing them.

NO SURPRISE INSPECTIONS

"Education is a progressive discovery of our own ignorance."

Will Durant

CASE OBJECTIVES

- ○ To reveal some of the typical challenges involved in a cultural change
- ○ To understand that true behavior must be revealed before effective, planned, cultural change can begin

CONTEXT

You have just accepted the position of Safety Manager for a company. In your initial visits to the company facilities in the United States, you become convinced that there are numerous safety violations occurring on a daily basis. You meet with the CEO and propose a safety program to be rolled out and a series of no-notice inspections to be carried out at several company facilities over the next six months.

The CEO does not agree with the practice of no-notice inspections but agrees to accompany you on a series of announced visits.

- ○ **What is behind the actions of the CEO?**
- ○ **What are your options as Safety Manager?**

The CEO feels it would be demotivating to carry out the no-notice inspections. He agrees to a program of safety training to be conducted over the next few months, but continues to hold to his position of prohibiting no-notice inspections.

- ○ **Can you succeed in transitioning to a safety culture with "announced" inspections?**

TOXIC OR JUST TRUTH?

"Truthful words are not beautiful; beautiful words are not truthful. Good words are not persuasive; persuasive words are not good."

Lao Tzu

CASE OBJECTIVES

- To enable participants to differentiate between toxic and truthful speech as leaders and followers

CONTEXT

The Marketing Director of a British company is visiting the US offices. He has a brusque and demeaning manner and does not engage in conversation readily. A newly hired Business Operations manager has just gone through a difficult divorce and a time of unemployment. He is grateful to be working in the field again. On his first meeting with the Director, he expresses his thanks to him "for having confidence in me and hiring me". The Marketing Director replies that ". . . James, I have no confidence in you at all. Whether or not I will ever have confidence in you remains to be seen. I have confidence in Bill (the US VP of Operations)". He then turned and walked away.

- **Discuss the Lao Tzu quote as it applies to this situation.**
- **Are these words of the Director truthful?**
- **Could he have phrased the response differently, especially on his first meeting?**
- **What indication of his style as a leader do his words give us?**

AN ENGINEERING PROBLEM

"Risk comes from not knowing what you're doing."
Warren Buffett

CASE OBJECTIVES

- ○ To display the importance of taking risk when situations are appropriate
- ○ To demonstrate the fact that sometimes leaders may help from followers with respect to technical issues

CONTEXT

You are an implementation team leader for an industrial control system application. Your client is a major company, and your responsibilities are to install the system and train the client personnel for a new packaging system. You have been in the role for several months. The installation went well, but now you are beginning to experience equipment problems which typically result in the loss of the control system computer in the packaging unit. You have heard of this problem, but have never personally experienced it. One evening as you supervise the night shift implementation team, the control system on one of the newly installed units shuts down. Your manager is very competent and supportive, but he is not a technical type. He tends to be very strict with procedures and processes, and does not like to deviate without lots of discussion and proof. The problem you just experienced has been plaguing the company since the project started. While you are looking at the unit, one of the electricians for the client company walks by. You ask him to come over, and the two of you discuss the problem. He thinks that he knows what the problem is, and he offers to quickly rewire the supply circuits so that he can isolate the two principal parts of the unit and stabilize the power sources. You have studied the problem as it occurred in other units across the company, and you think that by testing the circuit you may be able to isolate the problem. However, your boss will very probably not like the idea of making such a field change, since the client engineers have been confident of their design, and he is reluctant to challenge them. You also suspect that he will have concerns about what to do if the problem is in fact a faulty circuit because that will require a re-design of the entire circuit and possibly the need for new power conditioning equipment to be installed, costing more than budgeted. You feel confident that if you isolate the circuit, you can solve the problem, but it's late at night, and you don't want to call your manager.

- **What are your options?**
- **What is "doing things right" in this case?**
- **What is "doing the right thing" in this case?**
- **Discuss the consequences, both intended and unintended, of a successful proof of concept, i.e., you discover the problem with the circuits and know how to fix it.**

The group leader and electrician made the change. It proved beyond doubt that the original circuit design was faulty. The group leader called the manager the next day. He was troubled by the change. The group leader told him that he would come up to headquarters in a few days and explain the problem and its solution. He sat with the manager and brought him up to speed on the problem, patiently explaining the basic physics and engineering applicable. The manager was now convinced that a solution was at hand, but still concerned about the response the client would have. The group leader offered to go with the manager to the client engineering group and explain the issue. The engineering group had done the initial design and would not be pleased. Together the client and consultant company worked out a cost effective method to fix the problem.

- ○ **It requires courage and often technical competence, along with an ability to teach, to solve certain problems.**
- ○ **Even bad news can sometimes be well received if delivered properly.**

COMMUNICATING DOWN INTO THE RANKS

"The day soldiers stop bring you their problems is the day you have stopped leading them."

Colin Powell

CASE OBJECTIVES

- ○ To demonstrate the importance of frequent and less structured communication in building a communications "bridge" with all levels of the organization
- ○ To illustrate the point that appointed leaders cannot always rely on their position but must instead actively seek to establish communication through trust

CONTEXT

You are one of several regional managers of a medium size manufacturing company. Your subordinates are five plant managers in several mid-western states. You have frequent meetings via teleconference with the plant managers, but visit each of the plant facilities about once a year. You keep in touch with reports, written communications, and telephone. Each plant manager supervises a local sales force, an operations group which runs the plant, and a logistics manager who moves product into and out of the plants. You know the names of many of the people at the plant level, but you do not have a regular opportunity to communicate with them on a personal level.

At the present, both your plant manager and his immediate reports are attending a training conference in another city. During this time you hear of serious problems at the plant, and learn that several key production personnel are planning to resign. Without informing the plant manager and his subordinates, you schedule a trip to the plant to discuss the matter with the employees.

Once you arrive you ask each of the employees to spend time in private with you so that you may learn of the problems and their reasons for planning to resign. To your surprise, none of the employees wishes to discuss the issues, and they each say that while there are problems, they believe that things will work out. Perplexed, you have no choice but to make the trip back to your office empty handed.

- **Why have you not learned of the reasons for the discontent of the employees?**
- **What possible motive may have prevented the employees from talking more freely with you?**
- **What steps will you take now to improve morale at the plant?**

The regional manager was rarely seen in the field. Most of the employees knew him on sight, but had never spent time communicating with him, especially on a one-to-one encounter. This made them uncomfortable, and reluctant to discuss the problems with him. He had never built a back-channel communication with these people, and they were afraid to discuss the issues for fear of retaliation from the local management. This case illustrates the need for frequent communication at all levels if we wish to lead effectively. The best way to do this is for the regional manager to schedule visits where he spends time "on the job" with the plant people, drivers, production managers, and assembly workers. In this way, he will build trust and a channel of open and honest communications. This problem would be solved very differently in the military. In that environment, it is common for Field Grade Officers to visit the troops at work, and to solicit information and to communicate freely. This is a culturally established practice in the military, and it yields great results. It rarely works that way in civilian organizations for a multitude of reasons. A manager who is several levels above factory floor workers will be received cordially, but may not get the whole truth during his visit. The reason is fear of job loss. Only if the visits are established and part of the organizational culture will they yield honest and open communication. You won't have to go down into the ranks if you strive to build an upward flow of information rather than only downward.

KNOW THEIR STORY

> "Lead and inspire people. Don't try to manage and manipulate people. Inventories can be managed but people must be lead."
>
> **Ross Perot**

CASE OBJECTIVES

- ○ To acquaint the participant with the fact that personal issues tend to work their way into the system and must be attended to with frequent and significant communication

CONTEXT

On 1 November 2011, US Air Force General Mark Welsh addressed the cadets of the Air Force Academy.[35] In his speech he covered a number of topics on leadership but one in particular seems to stick. In this segment of his speech he talked about learning of a very serious family matter concerning one of his airmen, a senior sergeant. Welsh noted that he had a habit of walking the flight line and spending time with his people. He felt good about this and was satisfied with his leadership style. This problem had completely escaped him however, and it was only through emergency measures that Welsh succeeded in getting the airman home on emergency leave so that he could resolve the problem. Welsh lamented that though he spent much time walking the flight line, he spent too little time with his people in learning their story. He was of necessity concerned with work conditions, material conditions, and problems in the maintenance of their airplanes. His admonition to the assembled cadets was "know their story". How they perform is only part of their story. The events in and around their families impact their work, and the good leader knows this.

When Ross Perot was leading EDS, he had the reputation of descending on the cubicle of an unsuspecting employee to ask how his family was doing. Perot always knew whether there was something serious going on with the employee, typically a child or family member in the hospital. In one such story, Perot asked why the man was at work instead of at the hospital with his sick wife. The employee replied that he was out of sick time and vacation time. Perot responded ". . . we'll figure out how to deal with that later. Don't worry about it. You get to your family."

- **How does the action of CEO influence in this case?**
- **What might be the result of Perot's tactic on lower level managers?**
- **What message is he sending?**
- **Which is more effective, requiring managers to inform Perot of such situations through written policy, or having Perot lead by example?**

EDUCATION

THE K-12 SCHOOL AND THE TRANSACTIONAL PARADIGM

All of our concepts of leadership are shaped initially by our experiences in education. We may accept that the military imparts a stronger and longer lasting experience of leadership, or that the many years we will spend in a business environment will mold our concepts of leadership, but early experiences can be very dominant in the formation of our approach to leadership.

The case can be made that the transactional paradigm begins at birth with the parents of a child. But after only a very few years with parents and the most basic of socialization skills, the child enters the formal and highly structured environment of the school. For most of these children, it is a process which will continue for twelve years, and for some, longer. Whether or not young people emerge from those first twelve years having experienced the model of transformational leadership is largely dependent on school administrators and teachers.

As a society, we place importance on the school as a transactional event. There is a system of instruction with benchmarks for completion. The student must respond to varieties of subject matter with multiple teachers. With the exception of personal risk, it is a paradigm which compares closely to the military model in many respects. Once a young person enters the school system, the school becomes the place where most of their time is spent. Teachers compete with action games, different first languages, cell phones, a celebrity-oriented culture devoid of ethics and values, violence, absent parents and broken families. In spite of all these challenges, they are tasked first with attending to the transactional values. Standard tests have become the fashion in many school systems, thereby establishing a discrete numerical indicator which may not tell us much about the emotional and psychological value of the total experience.

This array of challenges begs the question whether or not leadership of the transformational type is even possible in a school setting. Ironically, experts and researchers in leadership are coming to the conclusion that leadership cannot be taught, only learned. Some educational administrators who are well accustomed to the didactic process are perhaps ill suited to the creation of a transformational leadership environment in their schools. Many are comfortable with the quantitative benchmarks as the only criteria for success. Over the years of observing my children and others in both public and private school settings, I have found some administrators who actually prevent good teachers from embracing a leader role. Despite the challenges of developing such an environment, we cannot shrink from the problem. There are adequate models from which we may gain a better understanding of transforming schools and students. It is imperative that we create a cadre of administrators and teachers who embrace the leadership paradigm and are dedicated to its application. We have to move from the straightforward bottom line of the transactional in schools to learn how to develop systems that actually transform and generate the critical thinking skills students will need to compete.

Zero tolerance policies promulgated in many schools are the result of changes in economies of scale in schools. Bigger classes, bigger schools, and the proliferation of zero tolerance are the bureaucratic result. These policies simplify the process for school administrators and teachers who have no feel for true leadership. The result is the production of huge numbers of students who have experienced a rigid and transactional system which often saddles them with criminal charges while still in school. [36]

A NUN AND A BOMB

"Courage is not simply one of the virtues, but the form of every virtue at the testing point."

C. S. Lewis

"Instinct is action taken in pursuance of a purpose, but without conscious perception of what the purpose is."

Van Hartman

CASE OBJECTIVES

- To grasp the importance of instinct
- To advance the importance of personal bravery

CONTEXT

The year is 1955 at a small Catholic school in the south. It is recess and a group of boys are tussling, playing. There is a boom, the ground shakes, dust flies, and one of the boys begins to scream in terrible pain. Students on the playground are stunned, shaken. A nun suddenly gathers up the skirt of her habit and rushes to the two fallen students only to see horrible damage, blood, bits of flesh on the ground and a smoking hole. She dispatches students to the office to call for help, and remains with the two students, one of whom is wounded terribly and in immediate danger of death.

- **Discuss the role of instinct in this case and how it relates to other similar situations.**
- **Why is it that we often tend to rush instinctively into such situations? Does this "rush" indicate the presence of a similar need that is not demonstrated by sudden tragedy but is always present in less obvious ways?**

The student who was most seriously injured lived near a railroad track and had found a device used by conductors to signal when the train reached the limit of a siding. The local term was "railroad torpedo". The device consisted of a block of explosive with two electrical leads. During the tussle the leads connected and the device exploded producing a devastating wound similar to a grenade. The student needed reconstructive surgery to save his leg which was broken in multiple places, and he lost a tremendous amount of blood before he reached the hospital.

Instinct is a basic human emotion. The sheer bravery of this woman who rushed into what might have been personal danger to see the carnage was remarkable. She was poised and calm and served to provide stability both during the crisis and after, while the school followed the course of the injury over the next several days. Leaders provide this kind of calmness even in the midst of terrible chaos. I witnessed this event and the chaos afterward. It influenced me greatly and taught me, in an instant, what is sometimes required of leaders.

DON'T TEACH TOO FAST

> "Be a yardstick of quality. Some people aren't used to an environment where excellence is expected."
>
> **Steve Jobs**

CASE OBJECTIVES

- ○ To demonstrate the importance of transactional standards and their application
- ○ To show how some leaders will take the easy but wrong path rather than the hard but right path

CONTEXT

A teacher notices that students entering his advanced classes are poorly prepared, and often have covered only a few chapters of the curriculum standard required for the basic courses. When he brings this up to an administrator, he is admonished for "teaching too fast", despite the fact that his success rate among students is very high, and his classes are well motivated and disciplined. The teacher in the basic courses has been accomplishing about half of the lessons required for meeting the prescribed standard in the advanced courses.

- ○ **Can you account for what is happening here?**
- ○ **What significance do the remarks of the administrator have for the culture of the organization?**
- ○ **For the students?**
- ○ **For the teacher of the advanced courses?**
- ○ **For the teacher of the lower level courses?**

The administrator wants the teacher of the advanced courses to slow down. In essence, he is asking him to lower his standards to the lowest common denominator. Leaders sometimes act as transactional managers when they revert to the desire for stability above change, and the desire for control above passion. Passion, excitement in a task, is a trait of true leaders. The teacher who is "teaching too fast" is achieving excellence for himself and most importantly, for his students. He is leading his students to a level of excellence, to achieve more than the minimum.

NOT ENOUGH WRITE-UPS

> "It is the mark of an educated mind to be able to entertain a thought without accepting it."
>
> **Aristotle**

CASE OBJECTIVES

- ○ To show how rules can poison the actions of a follower
- ○ To illustrate the true reasons for rules and other procedures

CONTEXT

A young teacher in an American high school is receiving an evaluation from her supervisor. During the course of the evaluation, which is positive overall, the supervisor notes that the teacher seems to have a significantly smaller number of students who have been "written up" for disciplinary infractions. The supervisor contends that the teacher needs to write up more students so that she will have the same percentage of infractions as other teachers. A discussion follows, and the supervisor is adamant that the teacher must write up more students. She <u>must</u> find more rule violations, and the supervisor then tells her that she should look for specific things, many of which are very minor.

- ○ **Is the goal to find infractions, or is it to have discipline**?
- ○ **If the teacher has fewer reasons to write up infractions, is she meeting the goal of discipline?**
- ○ **What might you discern about the culture of this school?**
- ○ **What suggestions do you have to effect change in this culture?**

This is a situation where a supervisor does not seem to understand the difference between the transactional "quota" mindset and the fact that the teacher has achieved a greater level of discipline among her students and has created a transformational environment. Many managers and administrators find great comfort in the mind-numbing exercise of finding fault. Perhaps this is because they are relieved of the burden of thinking by the process of fault finding.

THE AFTER PRACTICE SESSIONS

> "Good coaching is good teaching and nothing else."
> **Pat Conroy, *My Losing Season: A Memoir***

CASE OBJECTIVES

- ○ To demonstrate how influence and indirect leadership is used
- ○ To foster the application of indirect leadership when opportunities for it arise

CONTEXT

The football coach at the Catholic High School I attended had been a Marine Lieutenant who served in combat in Korea. At our ages, we had little concept of leadership. We participated in sports for the excitement and challenge. We looked up to the coach because he knew sports and because he was a firm but fair mentor who taught us the game.

One day as we were entering the field house after practice, he asked us to take a seat. He said he was beginning a series of after practice sessions that would have nothing to do with football, but which were things he felt we should know about the more important issues of life in general. His first lecture was on the history of the handshake, what it meant, and how people might judge us by our implementation of the custom. Later sessions would follow. They would be about the value of applying ourselves in our studies, proper language, respect for elders, and generally were directed toward making us young men who would be accepted graciously in the larger society beyond the school. The coach eventually pursued and was awarded a Doctorate in Education, and became

Superintendent of Catholic Schools in the area. He also won a great number of football games over several seasons.

- ○ **Analyze and describe the leadership approach of the coach.**
- ○ **Discuss indirect or influence leadership and its applications in organizations.**

PERFORMANCE ENHANCING DRUGS

"I am not a teacher, but an awakener."

Robert Frost

CASE OBJECTIVES

- To demonstrate the actions of a real life leader in a critical problem
- To provoke discussion on issues of ethics and responsibilities of a leader

CONTEXT

The Athletic Director of a University learns that a member of the football team is being investigated by the local police for involvement in the trafficking of drugs, after having been found with a large quantity of drugs in his residence. He decides that he will not wait for the police investigation to be completed. He begins his own investigation, and orders a mandatory testing of all athletes in the university, the suspension of the football coaches with pay until the internal investigation is completed and the suspension of the football season for the coming year.

- **What does this action by the Athletic Director say about his leadership?**
- **What about the athletes who were unable to play and were not using performance enhancing drugs? Was this fair to them?**
- **Are there any downsides to this action?**
- **What are the positive benefits of this kind of leadership?**

Leadership is distinctly different from other types of actions and sentiments. It is not a popularity contest. While certain leadership moments generate profoundly warm sentiments and followers, sometimes leaders must act in ways that seem harsh and counterproductive. This event was one of those times. It was not universally accepted as an event that was considered necessary, and some, especially players not involved in the drug use, were angry with the actions of the Athletic Director. There were angry statements by some that this Athletic Director overreacted, and that there should have been better ways to solve the problem. But leaders are different. They are often out in front addressing problems that others should have addressed. The Athletic Director made a strong statement. In this case, there were consequences for both athletes and the country's national body which regulates sports. By the action of the Athletic Director, a more aggressive and thorough testing program was instituted throughout the country. Leaders often act not only on followers, but as shapers of influence on other institutions, sometimes those to which they report administratively. Leaders are capable of acting in both directions, downward to followers, and upward to those who may have failed to act on their own. They fill leadership vacuums.

THE PRACTICE INTERVIEWS

> "True education does not consist merely in the acquiring of a few facts of science, history, literature, or art, but in the development of character."
>
> **David O. McKay**

CASE OBJECTIVES

○ To provide an example of a transforming experience within a very highly structured and transactional environment

CONTEXT

The English Department of a Public High School has a number of students who are recent immigrants. Often these kids have poor command of English and are overwhelmed by their new environment. Many come from single parent families. At the end of the freshman and junior years, the Department sponsors an interview day. Freshmen tend to be looking for summer work, and the juniors are often thinking of college interviews or jobs also. Students are encouraged to participate in practice interviews with three different groups of the local community. The largest group is from the business community, and participants also include police officers and military members. At one such session a young Army Staff Sergeant remarked that" . . . these events always turn into counseling sessions. They really are in need of role models." Students are taught to follow up in writing with thank-you notes to interviewers.

○ **Discuss this event from the perspectives of the transactional and the transformational. How does it address both?**

○ **Place yourself in the position of a student. What would you have thought of had such a program been conducted in your high school?**

○ **Can you make a distinction between this type of learning and the typical learning approach?**

○ **Explore the use of experiential learning in a typical school environment, and discuss the difficulties and challenges of the experiential approach.**

ETHICS AND LEGACY LEADERSHIP—
THE SLEEPING SURGEON

"Change is the end result of all true learning."
Leo Buscaglia

CASE OBJECTIVES

- ○ To reveal the strength of legacy systems and the difficulty involved in changing them
- ○ To recognize the ethical issues sometimes attending such systems
- ○ To establish the responsibilities of leaders and followers in events such as this

CONTEXT

A young surgical resident physician is in his second year of training since graduating from medical school. The schedule is physically demanding. He often rises before five o'clock and spends the morning before surgery making rounds, with the afternoon to following the progress of patients and other surgery if required, sometimes late into the night. This morning he is working alone in the operating room with only a couple of nurses and anesthetist present. He has laid open the abdomen of the patient, and the operation is fairly routine and no complications are foreseen. In his right hand he holds a scalpel and both hands are exploring the internal organs of the patient. He becomes aware of someone tugging at his left sleeve. It is the nurse. He has fallen asleep on his feet.

He brings the event up to chief resident in charge of the surgery program, telling him that he is concerned for the safety of the patient under such conditions, who dismisses the issue quickly.

- ○ **What is happening here?**
- ○ **Why is it happening?**
- ○ **Does the young resident have an ethical duty to escalate the problem to a higher authority than the chief resident?**
- ○ **What might you do in this position?**
- ○ **Does the chief resident have a duty? To whom?**

Legacy training programs are often difficult to change. The response of the chief resident to the physician was "I had to do it that way; I'm not going to change it for you". Programs such as this work only because of participants who despite the clear abuse are committed to making no waves out of fear. At some point though, accidents and incidents reveal the underlying problems. The fact that an accident occurs usually reveals the problems, but by then the damage has already been done. Asking why something is done a certain way is a right and duty to new leaders and participants in such programs. Courage and truth enable productive changes in organizations.

- ○ **Can you see opportunities in this case to implement the Schein model?**
- ○ **Which implementation steps might you apply in this event?**

LATE ARRIVALS AND SICK DAYS

"The more laws, the less justice."

German Proverb

CASE OBJECTIVES

- ○ To illustrate to leaders that certain rules have unintended consequences
- ○ To discuss the problems associated with proliferation of rules under such conditions

CONTEXT

This case was a personal experience. It happened when my youngest daughter was still in high school. Always a good student, she was also disciplined and courteous toward teachers. She had been at home for several days, having seen a doctor for a bad case of strep throat. I was home that week and not traveling. She had asked me to get her up early because she hoped to begin her classes again. I did so, but she said that she still felt bad. Perhaps an hour or so later, she woke, and decided that despite her malaise, she really needed to go to school. I wrote her a late arrival note and brought her to the school. When she came home that afternoon she was upset. She had been assigned a detention. It seems that there was a rule that any student who had an absence due to illness was not allowed to arrive late, but must miss the entire day or suffer a Saturday detention. The stated purpose of the rule was to prevent the distraction of a student entering a class late.

- ○ **We have discussed the use of rules in the transactional in other cases. What is your opinion of the use of the rule in this case?**
- ○ **What should be done about this situation?**

- ○ **What might be the motivational effect on the student if this rule is enforced? Will it contribute to transformational leadership?**
- ○ **Where does a parent draw the line here?**

In her case, she was making an attempt to do the right thing. I called the various levels of bureaucracy in the school with no success. "It's a rule" they said. I finally called the grade level principal and told her that my daughter was not going to be at detention, and explained my reasoning. I then told her that I would serve my daughters detention, and that I thought it might make a great news story. I then told her that I could not in good conscience allow the school to punish my daughter for having the initiative to get up out of bed and arrive, even if late, so that she could begin to catch up on her assignments. She did not yield, and I escalated the event to the school principal. He said that I should not worry; my daughter was not going to be at detention.

Perhaps the most important question to derive from this event is whether or not it is worth having a student miss the rest of the day because of a momentary distraction in the class.

There is a fine line here between blind advocacy of our children and making a case for a rule change. Our children had been told that if we believed they misbehaved, they would have to take their punishment, but this was a different situation which I felt strongly about.

If you are going to have rules, it is important to understand whether or not they have effects that may sometimes counter their purpose. We've established the need for the transactional, but sometimes it needs to be adjusted for events like this.

KURT HAHN'S TRACK MEET

"The doer alone learns"

Friedrich Nietzsche

CASE OBJECTIVES

- To demonstrate the potential for life lessons which are taught outside of the didactic setting in education
- To provide an example of leadership by influence

CONTEXT

Kurt Hahn was the German born educator and founder of the movement now known as Outward Bound. He pioneered innovations in education and experiential learning. In one of his stories about education he tells the story of his student's competition in a track meet. Initially, Hahn's students were sons of relatively wealthy parents, but later he instituted a scholarship program for needy students. In a track meet, Hahn watched as his students competed against a school whose students came from lower income groups. His athletes won handily, but Hahn realized that many of the poorer students competed in the running events without track shoes, and many were barefooted. This troubled him, and he considered the victory to be flawed.

- **What might Hahn do to even the field in this instance?**
- **Is the competition meaningful under these circumstances?**

Hahn saw the event as an opportunity to create a learning moment. He was not as concerned with the winning of an event as coaches sometimes are, but rather saw athletics as something that would work to improve character, and believed that any improvement in an individual's fitness or confidence was more important than victory. He asked the competing coach to consider a second event where the boys from his school performed without shoes.

- ○ **The results of the event are not known in terms of time and points, but consider the impact on the team from Hahn's school and their viewpoint on winning.**
- ○ **Discuss this impact as a leadership moment.**
- ○ **Consider it from the team which had no shoes.**

THE PHILOSOPHY CLASS VICTORY MARCH

"The only thing that interferes with my learning is my education."

Albert Einstein

CASE OBJECTIVES

- ○ To provide an understanding of how a symbolic gesture can change outcomes substantially
- ○ To provide an example of how thinking creatively contributes to leadership and performance

CONTEXT

A Notre Dame professor had the challenge of teaching a required course in philosophy for freshman students. He began to think of ways to make the course a bit less daunting for the students, most of whom had never had a course which compelled them to think analytically. He changed the mood by playing soothing music in the classroom. It generally worked well, and students tended to relax. On one occasion however, the scores on the test were terrible, and he realized that he needed to do something more to perk up the class.

- ○ **This professor seems to be an "out of the box" thinker. What might he do in addition to what he has already done?**

The professor did something very unusual and creative. Before beginning the test, he stood at the head of the class in a large room and paused. After a few seconds, the doors to the room opened and a large number of members of the Notre Dame marching band entered the room, playing the Notre Dame victory march. The atmosphere became electric as students began to stand and clap, and cheers filled the room as the band finally marched from the room. The professor says that every single student in the class outperformed their dismal first test scores, and he felt strongly that the emotional uplift provided by the band was the reason.[37]

- ○ **Why do you think that the grades were affected positively by this event?**
- ○ **What traits of leadership did the professor exhibit?**
- ○ **As you review and compare the attributes of the transformational leader versus the traditional manager, how many attributes of the transformational can you apply to this event?**

INDEX

ENDNOTES

1   Greek philosopher, from 490 BC-430 BC. Little of his writings remain, but he is often quoted in the work of others in the period.

2   *Managers can drive their subordinates mad"*: Manfred Kets deVries Harvard Business Review 1979, July-August

3   Burns, James McGregor. Leadership. New York: Harper Collins, 1978

4   Toner, James H. "Leadership, Community, and Virtue" National Defense University, Fort Lesley McNair, Washington, D.C. 1996

5   Malone, Col. Dandridge M. Small Unit Leadership, A Commonsense Approach Novato, Ca. Presidio, 1983

6   Fick, Nathaniel. One Bullet Away; The Making of a Marine Officer New York, Houghton Mifflin, 2005

7   Covey, Stephen. The 7 Habits of Highly Effective People New York, Free Press, 1990

8   Eugene O'Neill, *A Moon for the Misbegotten*

9   T.E. Weckowicz (1989). *Ludwig von Bertalanffy (1901-1972): A Pioneer of General Systems Theory*. Working paper

10 Stockdale, James B. A Vietnam Experience-Ten Years of Reflection Hoover Institution, Stanford University, Stanford, California 1984

11 Lewin, K. (1947). Frontiers in group dynamics: Concept, method and reality in social science; social equilibria and social change. Human Relations, 1 (1), 5-41

12 Tuckman, Bruce. "Developmental Sequence in Small Groups" Psychological Bulletin. 1965, Vol. No. 6:384-399

13 Bruner, J.S. et al. A Study of Thinking. New Brunswick, New Jersey: Transaction Publishing, 1956.

14 Snook, Scott. "Be, Know, Do: Forming Character the West Point Way." *Compass* 1, no. 2 (spring 2004): 16-19

15 Holy Bible. English Standard Version. Matthew 4:4

16 Martinez, Thomas. "Administrative Processes in Government" 11 September 2010 *http://www.csub.edu/~tmartinez/documents/INST%20275%20Syllab...*

17 Holbrook, Alexandra. Loyalty and the Sacramentum in the Roman Republican Army Open Access Dissertation and Theses: 2003 Paper 6500

18 Heraclitus of Ephesus. c 535 BC-475 BC. The Greek philosopher who was known for his doctrine of change as a constant. He also established the term "logos" as a descriptor of the source and order of the cosmos.

19 Schein, Edgar H. Organizational Culture and Leadership (San Francisco: Jossey-Bass 1985) 223-243

20 Hazard and Operability Studies-Developed by ICI in the United Kingdom for application in continuous process industries such as oil refining and chemical production

21 http://www.nwlink.com/~donclark/leader/want_job.html

22 As quoted in, Teaching Sport and Physical Activity-Insights on the Road to Excellence. Paul G. Schempp 2003

23 Crocker, H.W.III. Robert E. Lee on Leadership-Executive Lessons in Character, Courage, and Vision New York Three Rivers Press 2000

24 Shay, Johnathan. Achilles in Vietnam: Combat Trauma and the Undoing of Character. (New York Simon and Schuster) 1994

25 Roy C. Breaux, communication with author, 1966-1969

26 Col. Hackworth US Army,(Ret.) David and England, Eilhys: Steel My Soldiers Hearts, (New York: Rugged Land, 2002)

27 Chernow, Ron, Washington: A Life (New York: The Penguin Press 2010), 34

28 Fick, Nathaniel. One Bullet Away; The Making of a Marine Officer (New York, Houghton Mifflin, 2005)

29 Crocker, H.W. III, Robert E. Lee On Leadership (New York, Three Rivers Press, 1999)

30 Ford, Daniel. A Vision So Noble: John Boyd, The OODA Loop, and America's War on Terror. Greenwich, London, UK: Daniel Ford, 2010

31 Tom Wheeler, Take Command! Leadership Lessons from the Civil War New York: Doubleday, 2000

32 Rick Atkinson, An Army At Dawn: The War in North Africa, 1942-1943 (New York: Henry Holt and Company 2002) 33-34

33 Coram, Robert, Brute: The Life of Victor Krulak, US Marine (New York: Little Brown and Company 2010)

34 Detert, James N. and Trevino, Linda K., "Speaking up to Higher Ups; How Supervisors and Skip-Level Leaders Influence Employee Voice" Organization Science Nov. 6, 2008

35 http://www.youtube.com/watch?v=hFBpxB5zgnY

36 http://www.texasappleseed.net/Texas School Discipline Policies: A Statistical Overview

37 Morris, Tom. If Aristotle Ran General Motors (New York, Henry Holt and Company, 1997)

RESOURCES FOR LEADERSHIP

Alexander, Larry. The Biggest Brother: The Life of Major Dick Winters

Bentley, Trevor and Howard Boorman. Moments of Leadership: Leadership with a Gestalt Focus

Brennan, Joseph Gerard. Foundations of Moral Obligation

Brookhiser, Richard. George Washington on Leadership

Burns, James MacGregor. Leadership

Byrd, Martha. Kenneth N. Walker: Airpower's Untempered Crusader

Chernow, Ron. Washington: A Life

Crocker, H.W. Robert E. Lee on Leadership

Fick, Nathaniel. One Bullet Away: The Making of a Marine Officer

Flavin, Martin. Kurt Hahn's Schools & Legacy

Forsyth, Donelson R. An Introduction to Group Dynamics

Gellerman, Saul. Motivation and Productivity

Godfrey, Robert. Outward Bound: Schools of the Possible

Keegan, John. The Mask of Command

Kolenda, Christopher. The Warriors Art

Kozak, Warren. Lemay: The Life and Wars of General Curtis Lemay

Malone, Col. Dandrige. Small Unit Leadership: A Commonsense Approach

Marine Corps Institute. Fundamentals of Marine Corps Leadership

Montor, Karl et al. Naval Leadership: Voices of Experience

Morris, Tom. If Aristotle Ran General Motors

Schein, Edgar H. Organizational Culture and Leadership

Shay, Johnathan, MD, PhD. Achilles in Vietnam: Combat Trauma and the Undoing of Character

Simmons, Annette. The Story Factor

Stockdale, James B. A Vietnam Experience: Ten Years of Reflection

Taylor, Robert and Rosenbach, William. Military Leadership: In Pursuit of Excellence

Wheeler, Tom. Take Command! Leadership Lessons from the Civil War

Wilson, Renate. Inside Outward Bound

MOVIES

Master and Commander
12 O'clock High
We Were Soldiers
Saving Private Ryan
Lawrence of Arabia
Office Space
Schindler's List
Dead Poets Society
The Doctor
Invictus
Hoosiers
Money Ball
Band of Brothers (series)
The Longest Day
Rudy
Scent of a Woman (especially the speech of Col. Frank Slade before the committee (language))
Gardens of Stone
Apollo 13
Gods and Generals
Biography-Dwight D. Eisenhower

ORATORY

Col. Tim Collins on eve of Iraq invasion—
http://www.youtube.com/watch?v=UpdeNcH1H8A

Henry V speech before battle of Agincourt—
http://www.youtube.com/watch?v=OAvmLDkAgAM

MacArthur's "Duty Honor Country" speech—
http://vimeo.com/27105152

Winston Churchill "Their Finest Hour" Speech
http://www.toptenz.net/top-10-greatest-speeches.php

John F Kennedy Inaugural Speech
http://listverse.com/2008/06/01/top-10-great-historic-speeches/

Martin Luther King "I have a dream"
http://historywired.si.edu/detail.cfm?ID=501

Winston Churchill "We shall fight on the beaches"
http://listverse.com/2008/06/01/top-10-great-historic-speeches/

Ronald Reagan "Mister Gorbachev, tear down this wall" remarks at the
    Brandenburg Gate
http://www.time.com/time/specials/packages/article/0,28804,1841228_18
    41749_1841743,00.html

Patrick Henry "Give me liberty or give me death"
http://www.time.com/time/specials/packages/article/0,28804,1841228_18
    41749_1841743,00.html

Barbara Bush 1990 Wellesley College Commencement Address
http://www.americanrhetoric.com/speeches/
    barbarabushwellesleycommencement.htm

Lou Gehrig Farewell to Baseball-4 July 1939
http://www.artofmanliness.com/2008/08/01/
the-35-greatest-speeches-in-history/

Alexander the Great 326 bc
http://www.artofmanliness.com/2008/08/01/
the-35-greatest-speeches-in-history/

George Washington, **Resignation Speech, December 23, 1784**
http://www.artofmanliness.com/2008/08/01/
the-35-greatest-speeches-in-history/

WEB RESOURCES

http://www.nwlink.com/~donclark/leader/survstyl.html
http://hbr.org/2012/06/leadership-is-a-conversation/
http://www.forbes.com/fdc/welcome_mjx.shtml
http://www.leadershipinstitute.org/
http://www.nols.edu/